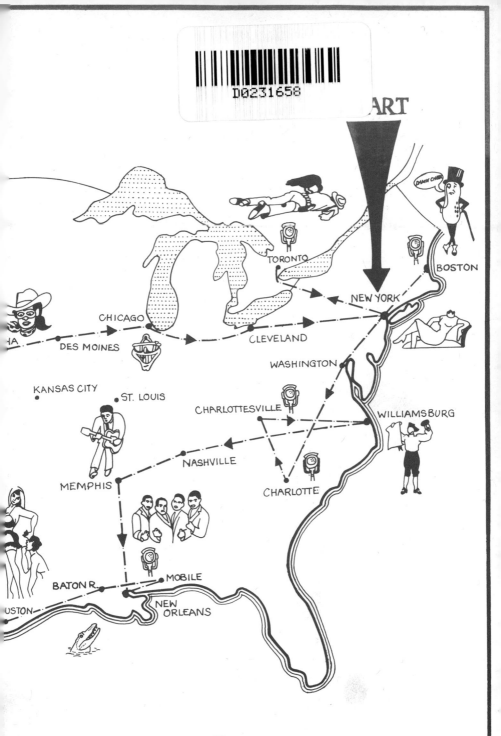

= POETRY READING

NO PARTICULAR
PLACE TO GO

NO PARTICULAR PLACE TO GO

Hugo Williams

JONATHAN CAPE
THIRTY BEDFORD SQUARE LONDON

First published 1981
Copyright © Hugo Williams 1981

Jonathan Cape Ltd, 30 Bedford Square, London WC1

British Library Cataloguing in Publication Data

Williams, Hugo
No particular place to go.
1. United States – Description and travel – 1960–
I. Title
917.3'04926   E169.02

ISBN 0-224-01810-8

Phototypeset in Linotron 202 Baskerville by
Western Printing Services Ltd, Bristol
Printed in Great Britain by
Butler & Tanner Ltd, Frome and London.

CONTENTS

ACKNOWLEDGMENTS

My thanks are due to Ian Hamilton for all his help and for publishing two sections in the *New Review*; to the *New Statesman* for permission to reprint 'O'Sullivan's Record Exchange'; to the following for permission to use quotations: Thom Gunn for five lines of 'A Crab'; Faber and Faber Ltd for two lines of 'Black Jackets' from *My Sad Captains*, and the poem 'Listening to Jefferson Airplane' from *Moly*, both by Thom Gunn; Jewel Music Publishing Company Limited, London, British publisher of 'No Particular Place to Go', words and music by Chuck Berry, © 1964, 1965 by Arc Music Corp., N.Y. (International Copyright Secured, All Rights Reserved, Used by Permission); and to Xandra Hardie and Neil Rennie for their many editorial suggestions.

1

FIRST STEPS IN NEW YORK

Any Minute Now and I'll Be Ready

I put a new blade in my razor and I held up my hand for steadiness. I covered my face with foam and I shaved back tiredness, old age and doubt to a bare minimum. I needed a really close shave this morning. Sometimes when I'm shaving I imagine a beard waiting for me in the future and maybe I shave a little too close . . .

I'd had my hair cut for America, but I hadn't worked out the parting yet, whether to use yesterday's or go for a new one. Some mornings all I have to do is run a comb through it and the hair makes up its own mind which side it's on. Other times I have to whip the whole lot forward and search for hours for the right opening. The angle of my first try was rather wild, but the parting itself was so clear-cut I decided to leave it.

So far so good. I chose my best tie and the knot came out right first time, the groove appearing on its own, as if from nowhere: a good omen. My shirt was light blue herringbone. I pulled on the narrow trousers and two-button box-back of a hard-wearing sixties suit. Then I packed the nine pockets with my survival kit: passport, traveller's cheques, return 'Pound-stretcher' to New York, pen, comb, lip-salve, address book. Any minute now and I'd be ready.

A Guest of the Sunset

'Ladies and Gentlemen for your comfort in the event of any

unscheduled flight modifications, buoyancy control packs are located on the underside of your posture supports, thank you.'

The man beside me fingers his Scorpio pendant and begins to smell of fear through his brushed denims. I drag my eyes away from the new penny sunset fleeing before us across the Atlantic and try once more to get beyond the first sentence of Kafka's *America*.

> As Karl Possman, a boy of sixteen who had been packed off to America by his parents because a servant girl had seduced him and got herself with child by him, stood on the liner slowly entering the harbour of New York, a sudden burst of sunshine seemed to illumine the Statue of Liberty, so that he saw it in a new light, although he had sighted it long before . . .

I got something in my eye at London Airport and it's still in there, making it hard for me to concentrate.

I see the back wing of the jet outlined against the vast swathe of electric light which is the coast of America. Then we circle casually like chairs over a fairground and bump down among the flares at Kennedy.

The yellow cab hurtles towards the city. Long silent cars bounce along beside us like slow motion motor launches, jockeying for supremacy. Sticks of neon express my happiness. We plunge into an underpass and up and there is Manhattan glowing black on dying embers . . . O take me there.

A Fistful of Addresses

Papers falling out of my address book as I stand in a windy telephone head-booth of the New York Port Authority bus terminal trying to find a bed for the night. This precious volume of distant friends and acquaintances took three years to assemble and is now disintegrating in my hands from sheer over-excitement. Why didn't I phone from home? I was trying to save on the bill by waiting till I got here . . . Now the lower East Side telephone exchange has been sabotaged by a fire-bomb. A picture of the disaster shows black-faced engineers standing knee-deep in smoking cables. The story tells of centres set up to cope with telephone refugees, the paranoids, agoraphobes, heavy-breathers, etc. There's a picture of some of them wrapped in blankets drinking hot milk like earthquake victims. My hosts, I dare say. I check my suitcase and look for something to eat.

Ten Minutes in America

Virginia Ham French Fries Baked Beans $3.10, 2 Knackwurst $2.60, Seafood Platter $3.25, Clam Chowder $2.40, Hot Pastrami Fries Bread Butter $3.10. Even the menu in this little Bar-Eats fills me with ridiculous happiness to be here at last in New York.

Danny Kaye on the tv: he prances eagerly backwards round a boxing ring, furiously pugnacious ten feet from his monstrous opponent. I laugh with delight at the thought of myself sitting here unknown and far from home, no work to go to and nowhere to sleep tonight, smoking untipped Chesterfields with childish glee as someone refills my coffee.

An ad for 'A little bit of old Ireland' comes on the tv and a cheer goes up. The black sitting next to me at the bar is ill-at-ease in this Irish nosh bar.

'Where's the black fella used to work here?' he asks.

'Abbie? Walking the dawg. Gravy, no gravy?'

Bright Lights, Big City

No phone in that Bar-Eats, so I've moved to a streamlined Chinese snack bar called The Columbus Diner on 8th Avenue. It's like an old charabanc parked in a vacant lot where children are still climbing on wire fences under floodlights. I'm sitting at the bar, phones behind me with stained-glass sunsets. Inside one cubicle someone has written 'To ask is to be excited. To be excited is to live.' Well, I'm so excited I can hardly dial the numbers, but when I try an actor friend of mine his answerphone says 'If you're phoning to tell me I'm on the late show I've gone to bed.' A slight chill there. I promised myself I wouldn't go to a hotel unless all else failed, but it's getting late now and they've just unplugged the juke-box. A junkie couple jig up to me, arm in arm, tearfully holding out an old watch, which I buy. It's time to go.

3

Shall I say I experienced some fear, standing in the street once more, with all this ignorance and indecision, the wind hurting my eye, and the great black city like a magnificent dragon snorting steam at me? No. New York seemed gravely, impossibly beautiful and I was happy to be lost in it for a while. I remembered how often the first view of a place turns out to have printed itself 'wrongly' on one's mind – back-to-front, too big, too small, the sea over there perhaps – and I wondered would all this change tomorrow.

I walked a few streets towards a hotel sign, then I heard some familiar music coming from a basement bar. I went inside and had my first American-measure dry martini.

Not Like That, Like This

'You know how to hustle?' said the girl.

'I can try.'

We made a place for ourselves on the dance-floor.

'Look . . . it goes like this . . . see? . . . no . . . not like that . . . like this . . . OK? . . . look . . . watch . . . right?'

I watched, but it wasn't as easy at it looked.

'Right . . . follow me, right? . . . one two, one two three, OK?'

I did my best but I couldn't get it to flow. My weight always turned out to be on the wrong foot. Her temper faltered.

'Look, I'll give you one minute,' she said reasonably. 'If you can't get it after that you're on your own, OK?'

'Try this,' I suggested, beginning the complicated doodle-step I do to more or less everything.

'Try this,' she said and left me in mid-step, buried deep among the calmly hustling people. Clearly this girl wasn't going to help me out. I made for the phone again. Why was nobody in? I had two more dry martinis and was deep in conversation with a mountainous wallflower lashed into out-size denims and chains. She said she liked my jacket and we talked about leather until Johnny turned up.

'Are you going to the party?' she asked me.

'Where is it?' I asked.

'Anastasia's. Don't forget now.'

'Where's that?'

'Lex and something – ask Johnny OK? Bye now.'

4

I walked down Lexington until I saw a crowd of people going into an apartment block. I followed them in, but they'd just gone up in the elevator. I asked the black attendant was the party here. No, he said. Must be down the street. I walked another mile and turned back. Was he sure it wasn't here?

'Is this Anastasia's?' I asked.

'Sure. But who are you?'

When gate-crashing in New York always say you were invited by Mrs Cohen, a friend had told me.

'I'm a friend of Mrs Cohen,' I suggested.

'All right then. You can go up now.'

I took the lift with a party of gays shrieking a kind of patois incomprehensible to me.

'You one of Rudi's?' one asked me.

'Yeah!'

Difficulties at a desk set up in the hall of someone's apartment to vet everyone's excuse for being there soon passed away and I was allowed into a homely after-hours club.

'Drinks are two dollars. But Pearl ain't here yet you know.' I walked into a bare room where about ten people were watching a lead guitarist playing alone. Deafening 'wee-wee-wees' expressed the longing of his soul for the other members of his group. I watched appalled as his knees touched. Lou Reed lay asleep on the floor. I wandered into another room where a bunch of people were sitting or lying on mattresses watching a video screen. The video screen showed the lead guitarist now playing to an empty room. Lou Reed's feet were just visible in a corner of the screen.

'You on your own?' said someone. 'Like you to meet Amy. Amy, this is . . . excuse me? . . .'

I told them my name.

'You English?' said Amy. 'My boyfriend's English. He plays with the Stones.'

'Is he in England now?'

'No, he's standing next to you.'

'Oh, ha-ha!'

'You a musician or anything.'

'No.'

Why are parties always more fun in the street before you get

5

to them? A gaggle of gays were getting ready to leave. There was a commotion as something valuable was spilt on the floor.

'That's Lou Reed over there,' sighed Amy.

'Is there a phone here do you know?'

'Through the hall.'

At last a phone rang somewhere in New York. After a long time Maggie came to answer it. Yes, she remembered me. Yes, I could stay. Take the cross-town subway.

Easy! I entered an unknown world of graffiti-splattered columns, hurtling graffiti-splattered trains.

'Don't take the "E" train', came to me from somewhere.

Do You Faint or Anything?

Maggie came to the door in her nightie with a prove-it-to-me expression on her crumpled face. I got out the duty-free Scotch, which seemed to appeal to her, and tried hard to make five o'clock in the morning arrivals seem groovy. Quite soon we were both drunk in different ways. Maggie slyly amorous, me triumphantly slurred. Dawn broke and we were just about to cuddle up in bed when we were suddenly treated to a demonstration of ecstatic gasping from the woman next door. The walls were paper thin and you could hear every creak of spring, every suck of breath from this apparently lone enthusiast. We stopped talking the way you do when a clock strikes. The gasps became moans. The moans became cries – then this invisible love-goddess came in a great bellow of what sounded like disgust at something she had just discovered in the fridge.

Maggie smiled secretly to herself and said softly 'She's great,' as of some much-loved entertainer. I felt rather sober. We had another whisky then climbed gingerly into the narrow bed we had been sitting on. My eye was watering profusely by now, mostly with alcohol.

'Where did I meet you really?' asked Maggie eventually.

'At the party for Twiggy, wasn't it?' I guessed.

'Was it? I remember your brother doing a trick, but I think I met you somewhere else. Do you know Warren Beatty at all?'

'No.'

'Didn't I help someone when you fainted or something? Do you faint or anything?'

'Look,' I said, 'I only fainted because someone was telling me

6

about how he trepanned himself with a dentist's drill. Would you like to hear about it? He gave himself a local anaesthetic in the skull. I was just trying to get to the window . . .'

'A friend of mine went to a Christmas party where they had real snow.'

'I think I'm beginning to fall asleep.'

'I've got my period, you know.'

The sex-machine next door was recommencing foreplay.

'Is it all right?' asked Maggie after a moment.

Oh it's great, I thought. I love blood everywhere. A Tampax thrown down like a gauntlet and something nasty in your shoe next morning. What more could one ask? I switched out the light. I had one of those tiredness erections which don't care what becomes of them so long as they aren't asked to get out of bed to pee. This seemed to be Maggie's condition also. She put her foot in the stirrup and swung a hungry leg over me. A forty yard dash followed by three hiccups and it was all over between us. I felt something warm trickling between my legs and wished I was back at the party.

Then came Maggie's verdict – a succinct phrase which I shall always remember in connection with my first sex-lag night in New York.

'I didn't like that,' she said.

My Op

At the eye hospital next morning they put my head in a vice and clamped my eyelids open with little golf clubs. Boris Karloff, grotesquely refracted in one of my tears, his face fringed with my eyelashes, approached my eye with a wooden stake. I tried to run away, but my head remained where it was. I couldn't even speak. Now the stake was apparently entering my eye. Unable to close, my eye was obliged to receive it. My body thrashed about behind me. My head remained motionless in its pillory . . .

'Souvenir for you,' said the kindly orderly.

The Robot-Monkey Fortuneteller

'I'm gonna piss on you motherfuckers . . .'

'Shit your eyes you little sister whore bitch . . .'

The yellowish blacks in silver waterproof trilbies mutter and shout at themselves on 42nd Street, scuff cheap boots in the slush. An old woman sits on a wall hungrily eating chocolates out of a heart-shaped box thrown out of a nightclub. A black soprano saxophone player sways to his lonely music outside the Phoenix Life Insurance. Here's an Orthodox Jewish couple out for a stroll. They look out of place until a big blue bubble appears at her lips like a mad speech balloon and she smiles at me like a good child.

Tacky shops on Broadway are scabs on the feet of glossy black skyscrapers that curve ignorantly into the air like perilous ski-jumps, the wakes of supermen. Watches, fortunes, porn: the shops purvey their solutions to a difficult world. One watch called a Hard-On has different positions depicted in luminous paint for every hour, and no time for sleeping. In the Pokerino Chance Game Arcade the robot-monkey fortuneteller picks up your fate-card and chucks it down a slide to you. I am 'Type D':

Success attends you and protection from physical danger. Do not push your luck. Your ambition is not the smallest part of you: hesitate before accepting assignments abroad. Make any changes in business after Thursday.

In Hubert's Wild West Museum I try to outdraw the Fastest Gun Alive, a black-clad, glass-eyed gunslinger with a hinged right arm which jerks upwards if you make a grab for the holstered six-shooter in front of you. I lose. Either way you lose your quarter.

From a roof-top ad for Marlboro Country a nonchalant cowboy blows real gigantic smoke-rings. 'I smoke for one thing,' suggests the Winston career girl. 'COME UP TO KOOL . . .'

A coach called the M41 Culture Loop draws up at all this squalor. Streams of yellow Dingaling cabs rush like white blood corpuscles to the latest wound.

Rona Barrett's Hollywood

The Circus-Circus is a convenience near Times Square. In its grubby window is the remains of a safe said to have been blown up by John Dillinger. Alongside a yellowing photo of this hero and a framed newspaper cutting of the day are some glamour

pics with the legend: 50c THEY CHANGE EVERY TEN MINUTES —
BEAUTIFUL GIRLS.

Inside, a dozen black men were lounging on pin-tables. At
the end of a central aisle a great black toad of a man was
perched high in a sort of pulpit, dispensing change to those who
wished to pass through a curtain into the holy of holies. I got
my 50c and went inside. The place was pitch dark and stank
like a urinal. As my eyes became accustomed to the acrid
darkness I began to make out the lower halves of men standing
in curtained head-booths with their backs to me. One of them
drew back the curtain to leave and I stepped into his place. Inside
the booth was a slot machine. I put in my 50c and a tiny screen
slid back, like the shutter of a lugubrious camera, giving visual
access to a brightly lit room where a naked white woman sat on
a revolving table opening and closing her thighs like a lobster in
an aquarium. On the floor copies of *National Stars* and *Rona
Barrett's Hollywood* were spilling out of a suitcase. Clothes and
shoes lay about. A French loaf protruded from a shopping bag.

You Don't Know Me, But . . .

'Let me get two slices of Sicilian,' said the man sitting next to
me in the Hot and Cold Submarines and Pizzas. 'I see ya got a
new air-conditioner, Alexi. They break in or what?'

'*He* broke in,' said the Greek, nodding to his young cook and
raising his eyes.

'Ladder slip on ice,' wailed the young man.

'Fried two with bacon all the way,' said the Greek, setting
down my order.

I was enjoying myself watching this team, but I had to find a
place to sleep for the night. I got out my address book. I had one
foot on my suitcase and a hand on a map of New York. Snow
blew in from the street. Obviously I couldn't go back to Maggie's. I tried the unknown 'Paula'. She didn't sound too keen on
the phone, but she said to come for a drink at her hotel.

Thai Silk and Tuna Fish

Paula was a delicate, determined-looking Australian girl, wearing a suit and glasses like the trusty secretary who knows she
will get a chance to be beautiful later when she is photographed

9

differently. My mother had known her father in Sydney. The other half looked Chinese.

We had three or four cocktails, then went affectionately in to a huge dinner on her expense account. She was selling Japanese animal reliefs to firms of office decorators. The 'he' in her life bought these in Osaka and shipped them to her in bulk. She put them into 'amusing' frames and took people out to lunch. We had this matter-of-fact kind of talk, full of highlighted truth. I told her about my childhood in the seventh floor flat of a stately home in Kent. She told me about her relationship with a Thai silk and tuna fish importer called Lord Jersey, who had given her this solid brooch of a clown. I showed her the scar on my hand, which she took hold of. By coffee I was telling her how I'd been thrown out of my room that morning and she was saying she didn't believe me but I could sleep on her floor if I wanted. On the way to the elevator someone gave her a message and she seemed to remember something. I wasn't really her type, she said, kissing me hospitably. I was mentally, I knew that, but not physically, did I mind? I said I did mind. She said I was cute but she was tired. I thanked her for the super dinner, arranged to break our next fondly made date, smiled martyredly and left, boredom seeping back across the rich food and forced fun of our four-course boasting match. She followed me into the street. 'All right,' she said, 'just for a coffee.' Once in her room we forgot the coffee and stood looking at the view of Central Park until the phone rang, her friend in Thailand, the clown. She asked him to hang on while she said goodbye to someone, did I mind?

Taxi to the Terminal Zone

My taxi driver has handlebar moustaches which you can see from behind. He twitches them prior to speech.

'You English?'

'How did you guess?'

'I lived there during the draft. Swinging London. You like a smoke?'

He puts the joint into the hinged money compartment set in the bullet-proof dividing window and tips it through for me. 'You want to have a drink somewhere? The name's Don.'

I haven't got anywhere particular to go, so I agree. Don pulls up at something called The Gaudy Image, 'The Only Place In The Universe To Have Anything to Offer on a Tuesday Night!' Inside, a group of waiters dressed as sailors flock round his moustaches for a moment. They look like women pretending to be men dressed as women. There are women here too, I think, but working on the opposite principle. These people are sexual palimpsests – often scribbled on but never coming clear, their genders whimsical. Half-coloured men in corsets and high heels flirt with secretaries in horn-rimmed spectacles. Half-female girls in suits and snap-brims pose on their own. The atmosphere is relaxed, self-absorbed.

'No one's straight here,' says Don, 'even him.' He nods towards a middle-aged businessman smoking a pipe.

'What about those two?'

'Men.'

Men? I looked at Don's handlebars quivering expectantly.

It is Amateur Night and we watch as an array of plumed and pasty transsexuals and vestites come through a curtain on to a tiny stage to amaze themselves and us with their bravado. The businessman comes on as Eliza Doolittle and does selections from *My Fair Lady*. His 'Wouldn't It Be Luverly' has a strange pathos which goes unappreciated. Most people seem to want to be Sally Bowles singing 'Life is a Cabaret'. One of these is Blue, who joins our table.

'Blue's got talent,' says Don insincerely. 'He's a bloody fine musician really, aren't you Blue? I've told him he's better off in London, but he won't listen. You want to go to London don't you Blue? Listen, Hugh, why doesn't Blue call you in London? You got an address? Look, I'll give you mine. If ever you need a place to, like, you know, crash, in New York or anything . . .'

He starts writing and I too get out my pen. As I write my name it comes to me that I don't want to give Blue my address. I've had a bit of that before. Anyway, why is Don in such a hurry to shuffle old Blue over to London? The trouble is I can't for the life of me think of a false address to give them. Without wanting to I find myself writing out my own address for this little creep. Summoning all my will power I manage to add an extra nought to the street number.

'Thanks, I'll look you up,' says Blue.

I make as if to leave, but Don wants to seal this contract here and now and insists that Blue give me a lift to wherever I am going. 'Great!' says Blue, beginning to get the idea that he has found a new patron. I say it's all right about the lift, but he insists. As we walk towards his car he chats warmly about the chances that bring people together. I try to disagree about this, but he doesn't hear me. He's talking about a friend of his called Sampson whom he met in a gents in Venice. I realise that I want passionately to be alone now. Blue scuffs his shoe and grins lovably at me. Why don't I mug him right here and now? That'd give me something to tell them back home. Blue, on the other hand, would probably misinterpret the gesture.

Ghosts of Electricity

For a few minutes in the thirties the Kennington Hotel was the tallest building in America. Now it's falling down. My room is extraordinary. One bare bulb switched on at midday. Is there a window? Not really sir. Frosted glass probably lets some light through to the other side, whatever that is. Thank you, I'll keep the curtains drawn. I can hardly breathe. Some rogue air-conditioner is dumping its used air in here. Lungs rake it in vain for oxygen and are left coated with a bitter dust. This dust has collected round the edge of the carpet like a pale border. There's the sound of a cat plucking at the carpet, but no cat. Cockroaches remain where they died, smashed, among the sinister flower-studies. In the bathroom someone has slashed the blind with a cut-throat. Electric shocks off everything. The cold tap comes on again if you turn it too far and the floor by the basin is too hot to stand on in bare feet. You keep your shoes on anyway in this place for fear of catching something between the toes.

So what? You want it regular you go to the Guardian Inn and get mugged. Just so long as they don't charge extra for the bleeding Village Person in the bathroom, I don't mind. At least the phone works.

Have Mercy, Judge

A St Patrick's Day newsfilm from Belfast, concerning the latest sectarian murder, has sub-titles added by NBC.

In the snow outside Grand Central Station an old black woman is selling green bowler hats with shamrocks stuck in the side.

A blind Irishman sitting opposite me on the Long Island Railroad has a telescopic white stick with TRUE TEMPER USA printed on it. He is neatly dressed with a real shamrock. Drawing himself up with some nerve, he addresses the blind air in front of him.

'I've always taken St Patrick's Day off,' he declares, 'and I always will.' The temptation to announce his nationality, holiday mood and status as a woking man, all in one phrase, is too much for him.

'Not even the Irish Irish take St Patrick's Day off,' says his neighbour.

'Well, that's their problem sir, not mine. Will you tell me, is it still snowing?'

'Sure is.'

The Irishman takes off his holiday homburg and lays what looks like a plastic tobacco pouch on top of it. Doesn't he know this is a non-smoker? He seems to be trying with his fingers to get the seam of the pouch in line with the crown of his hat. I long to help him but he fiddles it down over the crown and finally tucks the brim into the groove provided. Now he holds the newly fortified hat upon his lap and happily faces the whitening window, as a man does who is about to get down from a train. This blind Irishman exudes the good citizen. His every gesture is a kind of piety for conventional values, as if America has been good to him in his affliction. Even his hat looks satisfied.

We both get down at Westbury, Long Island, and I guide him along the platform in the gusting snow.

'English are you?' he asks. 'What brings you to this neck of the woods?'

'I'm going to see Chuck Berry.'

'Chuck Berry? Ain't he that fellow they got for income tax evasion? What do you want to see him for?'

'I like his music.'

'They should lock him up if you ask my opinion.'

His daughter lifts her eyes to heaven as she tucks him into her car.

The one taxi doesn't know where the concert hall is, so I stop another car and we're directed to a dismal concrete marquee at the back of a car park. It seems that 'long' really is the only word for this awful island.

I'm two hours early. I get my ticket and puddle-hop down the road to a Bowling. Inside, a desultory off-Saturday is in progress – sulky dads crossly sacrificing time at The Club to be with junior. I watch them busting their fat guts flinging cannonballs into nothingness – noise and light creating a momentary illusion of effectiveness, the shortlived satisfaction of something somewhere breaking because of them. Why do these big men look so disgusted with their lives and nag their kids like women overworked?

I suppose this is the America that surprises no one. Not the gallant USA of legend, but the America of half-baked panel games and enraged anchor men, whacky cleanliness ads and try-it-you'll-like-it trickery, the impotent, self-centred America of dumb hot-dog forecourts called Simple Simon's Big Deal or something, where you get a free dunce's cap with every suppressed scream. It isn't?

I sit down at the soda fountain and present my custom to the pretty waitress who might be a croupier or a masseuse or an air hostess she is so smart. The fat chap on my right doesn't think she's so fine and he snaps like a dachshund at the casual girl for flirting with his son, while his gratuitous belly commits hara-kiri on the edge of the bar.

'Two do-nuts,' he barks. 'Two shakes, one strawberry? Two strawberry! Christ!' He is posing sulkily like the Michelin man in his special reinforced bowling kit.

'Was that two nuts sir?' enquires the girl, looking straight at me.

'That's right honey,' sneers the man. His son comes round from behind the bar where he has been wicked enough to operate the milk whisk. I suppose this is a family scene where everyone knows everybody else except me – something one never thinks of. Maybe I stand out like an American tourist. I'm even writing postcards and not sulking and my eyes are bright for this soda-siren whose eyes are bright for anything.

'You wanna bowl or what?' I think the grotesque one is challenging me.

'I don't think I ever bowled before . . .'

'There's nothing to it,' he confides delightedly. 'Look, all ya gotta remember is this, right? First, ya gotta get your fingers in the right holes, OK? It's like a lot of things if you catch my meaning!!!' He laughs man-to-man, happy as a king now. 'Ya gotta be sure and stick ya finger in the right hole, ya know?' He's friendly enough I suppose.

'Name's Walters,' he tells me. 'Jim. Glad to meet you.'

We talk for a moment, then he tells me what's on his mind.

'Ya wanna know something? My son wants to be a road bum. That's right, a road bum. You ask him what he wants to do with his life he says a road bum. "Your lifestyle sucks," he told me the other day. Now what's that? Me, I save money for a hobby. My son says it sucks. He wants to be a road bum the motherfucker. He is a road bum for chrissakes . . .'

The phone goes and the waitress calls him over.

'It's for you, Mr Walters.'

He waddles over with one of the big cannonballs on his finger, glances at the ceiling authoritatively as he takes the receiver. A football coach? A sergeant-major? A ref? If he isn't in control of his life at this moment, he never will be.

'Yeah, Walters here. Hello hello . . . Oh . . . Oh . . . Yes dear it's me . . . Yes honey . . . OK honey . . . right dear . . . OK honey . . . OK honey . . . OK honey . . . Goodbye dear.' He replaces the receiver in severe depression: there goes his afternoon.

The Fat Man

Bored usherettes in green tunics to match the subdued décor flock eagerly towards each newcomer, all but one falling back when you show the colour of your ticket. The Westbury Music Fair has an arena stage which looks as though it's going to revolve. Chuck Berry, The Crystals and Fats Domino will be coming and going like creatures in a raree show. Yet there is no need – the place is only a quarter full, everyone is spread out through the empty seats, instead of together in the front. They are mostly schoolkids with nothing to do, nostalgic couples in special gear, some mini-rockers backcombing themselves, the odd black maid. Some fat white mums turn away their heads as they get up to let a pair of black girls through, but there is no tension here. Only a waiting to be amused.

'Ladies and gentlemen, the first half of tonight's entertainment will commence momentarily . . .'

The Crystals open the show with a bang. They do all their great Phil Spector hits – 'He's a Rebel', 'And Then He Kissed Me', 'Da Doo Run Run'. But the crowd aren't listening.

Fats Domino makes his entrance trotting down one of the aisles in the hope that the stage will be pointing his way when he reaches it. His clothes are more subdued than usual and he looks older. Antoine Domino was just twenty when he made his first rock 'n roll record in 1949. It was called 'The Fat Man' and the B side was in French: 'Hey là-bas, Amène vos chats'. 'Blue Monday', 'I'm Walking', 'I'm Gonna Be a Wheel Some Day', 'Be My Guest', 'Yes Indeed', he plays all my favourites, ending with a gospel tune called 'O Elijah' where he bumps his grand piano clear across the stage with his hip.

The Brown-Eyed Handsome Man

It is time for Chuck. He bounds on stage in red flares and Hawaiian shirt. It is one of those moments when a tourist understands what makes him an outsider. I have always thought of Mr Berry as one of the great poet-heroes of America, but to these kids he is just another old-time rocker, a figure of fun. Cries of 'Frankie Valli and the Four Seasons', 'The Mommas and Poppas', even 'Shanana' greet him meaninglessly, as if to give him a foretaste of their musical discernment.

'No Particular Place to Go', 'Cosy Clan of Four', 'The Promised Land', 'Maybelline', 'Nadine', 'Sweet Little Sixteen', 'Memphis', he does them all to a turn, dancing and grinning. The fact that he has done a blues version of 'Johnny B. Goode' earlier in the show doesn't stop the punk greasers in front of me yelling for it all night, but it doesn't bother him.

'Chuck, you're beautiful man,' cries a lone sympathiser.

'Just a voice crying in the wilderness oo oooo,' replies the brown-eyed handsome man.

> No particular place to go
> So we parked way out on the kokomo
> The night was young and the moon was gold
> So we both decided to take a stroll
> Can you imagine the way I felt
> I couldn't unfasten her safety belt

Riding along in my calaboose
Still trying to get her belt unloose
All the way home I held a grudge
But the safety belt it wouldn't budge
Cruising and playing the radio
With no particular place to go

Two nauseating boy twins in green satin party suits approach the stage to request the awful 'My Ding-a-ling'.

'You know I wasn't going to do this one,' he tells them. 'It's just a third-rate ditty really. But since it's been requested by the younger element . . .' and he does it with apparent zest.

At the end of the show he invites some kids on to the stage to dance and two of them sit down at Fats Domino's piano and drums and start jamming with him.

Why do I love these men? When I was five years old I heard a record on the radio called 'Tico Tico' by Carmen Miranda. It was fast. It produced dancing in me. I don't remember buying it, but I still have my copy. I was a pinched first-year public schoolboy when I heard the magical off-beat of rockabilly coming from a forbidden pre-fab called O'Sullivan's Record Exchange. That was the start of my record-browsing habit. John Lennon once said, 'I've been half American ever since I first heard Elvis on the radio and me head turned.' My case exactly. But the half is important.

O'Sullivan's Record Exchange
In the Peskett Street Market
Was out of bounds to Lower Boys
On account of Miss O'Sullivan's taste
In music. We used to jive
In the listening booths
When she turned the volume up for us,
Knowing we wouldn't buy.
It was the best she could do.
You couldn't hear that kind of thing
Any other way in 1956. The overloaded wires
Must have set fire to the partitioning.
They had to throw hundreds of
Twisted 78s into Peskett Street.

O'Sullivan's Record Exchange,
Its record-covered walls
Suspended in their own flames,
Still seems to welcome me
With all my favourite tunes –
And Miss O'Sullivan
Moving her arms over the turntables
Like one who heals. When I'm caught
Loitering in the new car park
Off Peskett Street ten years from now,
I'll know what to expect: 'Look here old boy,
The past is out of bounds, you should know that.'
'But sir,' I'll say, 'where else is there to go
On these half-holidays?'

2
SOME PARTIES

Come for the Filter. You'll Stay for the Taste

Mr Henriksen was the Agent for Readings. He'd told me he was balding, so I didn't look twice at the totally bald person sitting next to me at the Bar of The Collar Stud.

When I finally asked if it was he, he nearly jumped out of his skin.

'I really love poetry,' he told me angrily. 'I like poets. I understand them. You think I'm kidding. I'm not. I like Anne Waldeman. I don't like her poetry. I think she's a real sexy chick. I like her doing her readings. Would you believe me if I said that New York poets would honestly like for the next really great poet to be British? Or Australian even? I'd really like for him to be an Australian. I'd like to handle him myself.'

'I'd really like for him to be an American,' I said.

'I had a show in Sydney when I was your age,' said Mr Henriksen. 'Nobody came because they all thought I was going to smash up their cosy little scene.' He glowered round at the crowds of would-be pick-ups as if he'd like to smash up all the mirrors.

The Collar Stud is hunting lodge psychedelic – a sort of taste pause in which its clientele of sun-puckered divorcees, check-jacketed vermouth advertisements and wild-eyed cigarette-handlers of every persuasion can feel subtly refined. Outsize Aladdin's cave lanterns hover near one's head, giving off a sickly yellow gloom. Dark panelling causes claustrophobia. There is neither rhyme nor reason to the excesses cluttering the already tense atmosphere, but the place is filling up fast.

'How did it get this way?' I asked Mr Henriksen.

'This is the most popular singles joint in town,' he said. 'I been coming here ten years. I never got laid one time.'

'Why you go on . . . ?'

'The restaurant's OK. You can always say you're going to the restaurant, you know what I mean?'

I looked around at the nervous sportsmen with their shaving nicks and their tumescent ties, all presumably with a painful head of sperm built up between their legs, all imagining themselves doing something magnificently masculine to some grateful little lady later on tonight, but all looking as if they were just about to be tortured.

The whole atmosphere was far more discreetly uptight than the gay bar I went to, but the men, outnumbering the women ten to one, looked about the same. It seems that when Americans get cleaned up they all look like homosexuals.

'If my father saw this place he'd say it was a queer joint,' I said.

'He'd be half right,' said Mr Henriksen. 'They wanted to put it on tv, but the management refused. They knew it wouldn't be popular with the customers. Most of 'em are cheaters. Or would-be cheaters anyway.'

I smiled at a brassy hooker in sequins, but she raised a negative eyebrow and went blank. As in a gay bar, it seemed the glance was the currency, but more unstable, more wavering. You catch one, hold it steady, then give it a value with the response of your own eye muscles, releasing it back into the pool earlier or later according to the state of the market, which, believe me, isn't good tonight.

I looked round at the eyes looking round, at the efforts betrayed in scarves and cuffs – everyone in clean underpants in case of a voluptuous accident later. Here at last was a serious public for all the ads you've ever laughed at. These were the fashions they saw themselves being sexual in, which meant there must be women who responded to them. I noticed there were no jeans in The Collar Stud. The effort was clearly away from Bohemia and towards the Playboy Philosophy:

'Come up to Marlboro,' they seemed to be saying, advertising themselves in the manner of the cigarettes they were wielding with such dexterity.

'Taste is everything . . . If you know.'

'Are you Alive to Pleasure?'

And wasn't there a hint of sexual exploitation about those hearty jawline beards, sharks' teeth on chains? A suggestion of superior 'staying power' in those suede shoulder patches?

'Come for the filter,' they seemed to be suggesting; 'You'll STAY for the taste.'

Pelmanism

'Cigarette?'

'Thanks,' says the girl.

We light our cigarettes from the same flame, two synchronised fuses by which we guage the progress of our enthusiasm for one another. They go back and forth from our lips like sips of a shared poison.

Cigarettes are essential to the dedicated leisure cruiser. They are the Esperanto of casual sex, a kind of indoor semaphore, a flag of truce, a five-minute visiting card, an option on romance.

'My name's Lori,' says the girl, inhaling attractively. 'That means truck in English right?'

'Well, a small truck.'

'You moving to New York or what? I know a really good lawyer can get you a green card right away . . .'

'Well maybe I don't know.'

'You like New York? This is the most popular bar in New York. I know it's singles. That doesn't bother me. I like to get around. Hang loose.'

'You like to go somewhere after this?'

'You gotta car?'

'No.'

'I have to work in the morning. You know what I mean?'

The logic is international. We put out our cigarettes.

Mr Henriksen is nowhere in sight. It's after theatre time and the crowds are pouring into The Collar Stud like molten lava. They have shut the doors and are letting them in by turn, like a helter skelter.

A swarthy woman runs up and grabs me by the lapels:

'Ya gotta see *The Rocky Horror Show*,' she shouts.

'I seen it,' I yell.

'Isn't it the best in the world?'

I like her a lot, but I can't come up with any new feelings for

21

The Rocky Horror Show, so I have to throw her back. She tears up to someone else.

Is there some hysteria here? Certainly there is some hysteria here. Look at this one. Her head spins round as if she's possessed. She pirouettes alone, fiddling with her zip fastener, pushes through, blinking, smiles at no one, bursts out laughing, looks back. Now she's gone, but she's soon back again in dark glasses, looking for a light. There goes her drink. 'There is a neurosis in the air which its inhabitants mistake for energy,' says Charles Ryder about New York in *Brideshead Revisited*.

Two 'prepish' types (squares) are approaching a group consisting of two simian-featured blondes and their bait, a pretty Chinese girl. The Chinese girl sees what's coming and turns smoothly to meet a heavily spectacled older student type. He focuses his hunched shoulders full on her, but she is still a half-turn away from him, talking into the air. Soon I notice she is talking non-stop and his chest has started to swivel out of true. Is she trying to tell him something he doesn't want to know? I'd say it's a mistake to tell anyone anything in this bullring. Little by little he is turning away from this lovely girl, eyeing the blondes. Her explanation continues. Now she is facing him and he is about to have his back to her. He catches my eye and thinks I fancy his pick-up. He drinks heavily and turns back to her. There they are now, facing each other at last.

A secretary in pebbles smiles broadly at me. I look behind me. Maybe she sees me very clearly through those prisms, surrounded by rainbows. Maybe she sees into my heart. She passes in invitation, her white cardy open. I should hold up a card saying about 3. What happens to them at closing time, these swingers? Do they pair off quickly towards the end, as in pelmanism? Or are they knocked down to the cleaning staff?

I stop drinking Millers and enter a little run of vodka martinis.

I move along the bar.

Now here is a 'beautiful' girl in a mini-dress made of wet Kleenex. She has the scrape-back jet-set hairstyle. She is handling some money, but without any noticeable enthusiasm for handing it over to the barman. I invite her for a drink and she accepts, grudgingly. Her head is suddenly enormous. Her name is Kay.

After about ten minutes of trying I get the white Martini for her, but now she has got in touch with some new cigarette expert and they are discussing their respective packs with obvious lust for one another. The drink entitles me to have her turn from him to claim it and this she does. We talk for a moment about Stratford-upon-Avon. She wants to know exactly how long it would take her to learn to talk like me if she came to England. She asks me as if I have had this problem myself.

'What do you do?' I ask.

'I model. I broke my nose skiing.' This makes me realise she has had her nose fixed and her hair re-sprayed.

'Would you like to go on somewhere?'

'Like, I'm going somewhere, you know?'

'May I give you a ring?'

'A RING? Isn't it a bit early for that kind of thing?'

'You know, a call?' Just now a very tall man comes near.

'I wonder if he has a complex about it,' says Kay. 'At least he isn't horribly thin like some tall people.'

'No,' I admit. I am tall and thin.

Mr Henriksen comes up just in time. He says there is a loft party going on somewhere in the Village and why don't we all go. We can talk about my readings on the way. For some reason I thought he said a 'love' party and asked if there was a hippy revival happening in New York yet. That set us off on a longish cultural cross-purpose during which a new friend of Mr H., called Bruce, bought us all more drinks. Bruce was studying comparative popular cultures at Yale, so we all listened to him talking about the Beatles. Suddenly Mr Henriksen got quite worked up and told me angrily that I obviously knew nothing about the Beatles. By the time we had calmed down, picked up the girl in pebble specs and found our way over to Broom Street, the loft party was well and truly over and the lights out.

Judy, the girl in specs, seemed to have been taken under the protection of Mr Henriksen. I didn't like the look of him, but she had made her choice. Bruce had teamed up with a man in plaits, who wanted to smoke hubble bubble. The 'beautiful' girl had unfortunately slipped completely away with the tall man in his car.

I Didn't Realise It Lit Up

Tricia and I were acquaintances at least twice removed from

one another. I'd forgotten who 'Bobby' even was. I only knew someone called Bobby had given me her number and I'd written 'Bobby says chic' beside it. I called up and a voice said 'What's in it for me?' I was about to say 'Nothing' when I realised that this was the name of the company Tricia worked for. When I got through to her, 'Bobby said to give you a call while I was in New York' was enough to get me invited to a party she was giving.

'Chic' should have warned me. Despite her veil, Tricia was two steps back from glamorous, but her apartment was a disposable sensation. Eyes panned the zebra-print walls, did close-ups on prize-winning hunks of culture such as a brass-mounted elk's head, a huge blue photo of a Dakota airliner. All the doors had been removed from their hinges not to impede the invisible film cameras.

Did these people all know one another?

Was I the element of newness for tonight?

Now here was Tricia with a glass of white crème de menthe and a little pointed spliff pinched in a gilt-roach-holder. Who was I again? Oh yes, and what was I doing in New York *this time*? Nothing. Oh. Was that interesting? We passed smoothly enough into another doorless magazine feature where Tricia introduced me to a rich gay called Venus. The talk was of hiding places. There was a book published, Venus said, which told you where to hide things when you went out. Like round the S-bend in a net, frozen into your deep freeze, or round the neck of your Dobermann. I professed interest in this.

'I believe they got 30 per cent off all big dogs at the Pet Palace this month,' Venus told me.

'Not any more, they haven't,' said someone. 'They had a break-in. Took every dog in the place.'

This woman had a shop selling stuffed animals, she said, and these were discussed as an alternative deterrent to burglars. I thought this seemed pretty zany, but when I asked where the shop was the woman looked at me coldly.

'We don't let in any single men whatever.'

'Why not?'

'Too dangerous.'

'Who do you let in?'

'Single women.'

'I see Man was made the State animal of Connecticut over

24

the Bald Eagle . . .' said someone, attempting to change the subject.

'I thought it was the sperm whale . . .'

'My raccoon made an ad for Butterkist . . .'

The conversation was losing me. I was beginning to get the impression that these people's brains were saucepans full of boiling peas. I wanted 'out' as they say.

'Love your tree, Trish,' said Venus when the conversation had run out of animals.

'Jean-Pierre did it for me,' said Tricia. 'You MUST meet Jean-Pierre. You won't BELIEVE his eyes.'

'Do you mind my asking . . . ?'

'Two, darling. But he's not making any more right now.'

Two what? I thought. Two dollars seemed cheap for a perspex Christmas tree. Surely she didn't mean two hundred? No, she didn't. She meant two thousand. I asked and she told me. And that was the end of me. A light was switched on. Someone made a telephone call. His girlfriend came back into the room with her handbag in the shape of a poodle. It was late. We were tired. I wasn't, but everyone else was. A complicated dance of promises and endearments was performed under the desired tree, which now showed itself able to light up.

'I didn't realise it lit up,' I said to Tricia, by way of an apology.

'Oh didn't you?' she snapped. 'Jean-Pierre has worked for the City Slickers, you know.'

I asked some girl which direction she was going in and she answered loudly that she wasn't going in any direction as it was her house.

'Oh, you live with Tricia do you?'

'No, as a matter of fact I don't live with Tricia. I share the condominium with her.'

'The condom-what?'

'Minium. The apartment house. Goodnight now.'

We were drivelling forth into the night. Dimly I heard my name called by a group of guests who had found a taxi by turning right out of the door. I waved confidently from the darkening street-end. It wasn't until I saw the East River ahead of me that I realised my mistake. I saw something moving in a doorway and as I peered at it a man flattened himself against the wall. He had a piece of wood in the rough shape of a rifle, which he pointed in my direction. He was clearly terrified, a terminal paranoid. I put my hands in the air and went back the way I had come. 'A wise decision, darling,' said Howard later.

For wasting another evening and myself I forced myself to walk all the way home in my pointed boots.

'What is the meaning of this voyage to New York? What kind of sordid business are you on now? I mean, man, whither goest thou? Whither goest thou, America, in thy shiny car in the night?' (Carlo Marx in Jack Kerouac's *On the Road*)

All Through the City

In this mid-town garment district the street lamps are so high up that their meagre light barely percolates to the puddles of melting snow reflecting shapes of cars and bins of sodden off-cuts. In the darkened windows of wonderful taxidermist-cum-furriers, stuffed toads, two-headed cats and terrified indeterminate quadrupeds who have forgotten their far-off continental origins, stare out with a quizzical and dissatisfied glare. The people are so few and small and far between they hardly seem to inhabit these majestic canyons. Here and there a mobile telephone unit glimmers in the distance like a lightship moored on a lonely sea. The talkers stand in rows of six, their human trousers cut off at the knee by the cowling, their feet anchoring them to their loneliness in this empty late world, their shoes too old, side by side yet apart, while their dogs dangle from leads like failed nerve grafts. These are the telephone refugees, the telephone-less, untelephoned aboriginals without rights, the muttering, paranoid muggers and muggees, the druggers and druggees who never quite got the hang of it all.

Look: the mad cyclist again. A wild-eyed stranger with photos of Hiroshima on a pole and books about the Nazis pinned open on his back. He moves so fast you never get close enough to find out if he's for or against what he's advertising. Eyes on stalks and not a second to lose, he's off between the traffic as if men with scythes were after him.

Young, Gifted and Gay

A call from Tricia, being efficient. She felt sorry for me the other day. I'm to ring Howard. His friend is in Europe. He has a spare room. He's gay but I'll really get on with him. When I get there Howard is fixing one of the vicious little reefers they smoke all the time in New York. I sit at the table and this little twist of paper pins me to my seat for the rest of the day, words everywhere, my eyebrows reaching for my hairline as if their life depended on it.

This Howard is a specimen all right, a hothouse bloom whose tallowy roots tangle in the shallow earth of Welfare and the odd acting job for children or radio: competitive, desperate, weak. At eight o'clock he declares it is time to start getting ready for The Evening, The Life! He retires to the bathroom where a cat-tray is in powerful evidence. My own room, I notice, is equipped with a door which will not close properly. The cat, too, has remarked this.

An hour later Howard emerges with a hairdryer, fluffing his inadequate hair into the right mod bouffant. Now his skin is being scrutinised in a magnifying mirror and a thick layer of foundation cream applied to the faulty areas of his sallow cheeks. He has pink-eye and wants me to help him put in the drops. He leans his head back and opens his mouth in a perfect parody of surrender, murmuring grateful endearments. My hand shakes and the drops course down through his make-up. Now he puts in the contact lenses and his little blue eyes start smarting and watering all over again.

'But what am I going to WEAR?' he cries.

'Something warm anyway.'

'You must be joking, sugar. This is Saturday you know.'

'I'm wearing this.'

'I wish I looked like you. So English! My father is supposed to have been English. Are you gay?'

'No I'm not.'

'I'll ring Bambi. You'll love Bambi. Bambi's a coloured chick. You like coloured chicks?'

'Love them.'

He disappears for another hour or so to consider his wardrobe, leaving me in the company of his sex-demented cat. This animal sits in Howard's chair and all but rolls another joint. She screams directly at me.

'Don't scream at me,' I end up saying.

'Scream Scream.' Now she makes a heavy pass at my foot. I kick her across the room and she screams at me for more. I wish we could get out of here. But Howard is far from ready. Now he emerges backwards out of the bathroom, head cocked, to get a long shot of himself in the bathroom mirror. French sailor seems to have been imposed on the basic out-of-work cowboy. He has on a floppy black artist's beret, a striped T-shirt, white lace-ups. His hand-ripped jeans seem to attach to his bony thighs by magic. The zip itself has been completely unpicked down one side, affording visual access to pale blue undies.

'Well, what do you think?' he says, twirling for me. I see another strip of denim hanging down the back of his thigh as if a dog has had a go at him.

'You look very nice.'

'Young, gifted and gay,' says Howard happily. 'I'll phone Bambi for you.'

'Hang on, what's she like really?'

'My favourite black chick . . .'

This from Howard doesn't mean a lot.

Bambi is no sooner summoned than ringing the doorbell. A sorrier instance of darkie womanhood it would be difficult to imagine. She stands there, a sort of fat, retarded schoolgirl in a loose-fitting brown wig and dungarees, also loose-fitting, giggling uncomprehendingly at Howard's high verbal twitchings. Sounds like cries come out of my mouth. Thank God Howard is ready and we can leave. From an embarrassed hallway we conquer the street at last.

Gay, Black or Paranoid

First stop is the apartment of Julius. A burglar-proof door-prop is removed from its notch three feet into the room, then hurriedly replaced. Joints are enthusiastically prepared and inhaled. Jokes soon follow. 'London has ideas, New York gossip' goes the saying, but I couldn't understand a word of this Firbankian shorthand.

'Johnny! The Arthur and Bunny Joyce Hour!'

'Sitting on Arthur's knee . . .'

'Remember Bunny sliding down the banisters in *Cinderella*?'

'I thought Bunny was gay . . .'

'So did Francisco . . .'

'Where are you Pearl honey . . . ?'

'Coming you lovely big policeman you . . .'

'Start without her . . .'

'Flower, I didn't know you cared . . .'

A pause, pointed at me. I have been hoarding my cool by paying lavish attention to the music. But the faithful Howie is still hoping to squeeze a few points for escorting this prize Britisher.

'What was that you were saying earlier about gays and blacks, Hugo?'

'In New York you're either gay, black or paranoid.'

'Or else all three,' says Julius, 'Like Jeremy!'

'O my Gard!' says someone called Sombrero. 'That's amazing: gay, black or paranoid. Which are you, Saul?'

'You know very well I'm black, Sommie.'

Bambi squawks at everything.

Country Gentlemen

If straights like 'a bit of the other', I suppose gays could be said to go for 'a bit of the same'. They certainly do at The Ninth Circle. The couples here are smart mirror-images of one another, right down to the lock of clean hair. No rough trade here, no furtive glances. This is Gay Establishment and these are decent young Americans doing what comes naturally: prime stock in twills and tweeds, sensible shoes and sports jackets. Butch is the word. As befits his newly acquired status of normality and conservatism, this year's young queer is a country gentleman. Before I left England I got my hair cut short not to be shot-gunned while hitch-hiking. Now I find it's the badge of the new 'straight' sissy-loathing gays, the Marlboro moustache set.

The others have plunged into the crowds of friendly arms. I turn gratefully to Bambi, who loves everything and everyone.

'How did you meet Howie?' I ask.

'He was going out with my brother.'

'You work in New York?'

'I'm a maid three nights a week and I clear up after retarded children. But I want to be a singer. I write poetry. This is a photo of me singing with the Young Gospel Chimes. I was with the Thrashing Wonders before that. I used to clean for the priest, who's a friend of Sommie's. Now I clean for Sommie. That's how we all met up. They're my best friends now.'

'You don't have a boyfriend?'

'I had a little boy, but he's retarded. He's in a home. I like the gay scene now.'

I looked round for the others. Unhealthy eye contacts are strung like a web of tightropes in this cramped cocktail lounge. They warm and cool and flicker and they go on longer than man-woman ones. You stumble into them wherever you look and feel daft to have nothing to signal back.

A waiter touches my head to make way and I jump round like a hare. This seems to be an uncool place for me. I must wriggle out of it. I find Howard perched daintily on the knee of a moustachioed Hercules in Lederhosen. Goodnight Howie. Goodnight Bambi. Goodnight goodnight goodnight.

Life After Midnight

What shall I do now? It isn't even tomorrow yet.

The Curzon isn't a singles bar as such, but it is very cruisy: massive mahogany bar, gilt frames, darkened mirrors, burgundy or was it green drapes? It's the lobby of some old apartment block fashioned into a cocktail lounge for the rhinestone cowboy set. And it closes at two on purpose so that these husky cow-hands don't start doing kinky things in the toilets.

I'm fascinated by the size and effect of dry martinis and three have opened my eyes. Did she wink at me, or did I wink at her? And why didn't her boyfriend mind? Here she comes now round the bar, presents herself for speech. This young lady is completely drunk. She has very short hair, big drunk eyes and a piece of glitter round her neck which has left a mark. She has silk pyjama bottoms on with no knickers. She drops her gloves, then her bag, then her whisky. Already she is buttoning and unbuttoning my jacket.

Oh God, here comes her escort. He greets me with a friendly self-introduction and invites us both to a party. That's very decent of him, but I can see this young thing isn't going to make it. Mister nice-guy has seen a convenient loophole in the evening and he's playing his cards correctly. I buy everything he has.

Denise works in Vidal Sassoon, she tells me. That's about all she can remember about herself, except that she is a girl. She tries to get me to acknowledge this fact on the floor of the taxi back to Howard's place.

The next problem is the dormer bed which seems to function with the aid of various springs and levers which make my head spin manipulating them. Done properly, a secret, spare bed springs up next to its parent bed, forming a double one. I get it to work and Denise sits down heavily, looking dazed.

When I come back from the bathroom Denise is sitting on the guest half of this dormer bed, but it has collapsed under her, apparently without her realising, and is in the process of withdrawing once more to its position under the other one, probably from embarrassment. Wearing only a short mauve blouse Denise looks like a road accident victim, suffering from shock. I want to put a blanket round her shoulders. The bleak spotlights and quiet of my bare room have wreaked a sobering effect on our rush to climax. There is a ringing in my ears from another world.

'Where are we?' asks Denise.

'In my apartment.'

'Where's your apartment?'

'At 95 and Lex.'

This address is definitely counter-romantic.

'My Gard! I taught you lived near the bar!'

'I'm sorry . . .'

'You're not American . . . ?' She looks suspicious now. This is beyond her reckoning for a night on the tiles. She leans over to switch on the reassuring tv. I have to tell her it doesn't work. She asks if she can use the phone and I tell her that doesn't work either. Then I fix the bed by putting a chair under it, put out the light and climb over her into bed.

Why Her Boyfriend Didn't Mind

The rest of the night is cloudy in my memory, but I do remember that it had at least one more surprise in store for me. This girl had breasts like cannonballs. Not big, but inflated to bursting-point. As I ran my fascinated hands over these curiosities I realised they must be the much-talked-about silicone substitutes. There they were, stuck there on her chest, hard as a rock, with their poor little nipples marooned on top of them like little

31

rubber lighthouses. This idea Denise had of herself as an inflatable darling was going to wreck my impromptu character-
isation. Suddenly she seemed all too human: just someone's
little girl with a built-in sense of inadequacy. I was going to
have to think fast to overcome these plastic passion-killers
sweating coldly under my palm.

I cast around for the right erotic 'peg' to hang the occasion on
and remembered Apollinaire's necrophiliac nurse in 'The
Debauched Hospodar', grinding on the final erections of young
soldiers fatally wounded in the Crimean war. This seemed to
redress the balance.

In the morning I unplugged D's left nipple, rolled all the
drink-laden breath from her imperfect carcass and returned her
latex remains to the envelope marked ON APPROVAL.

'Just exactly where do you think you are?' shrilled Howard,
putting a tousled head round the door. 'This isn't a brothel you
know. You walk out on a good friend of mine. I do my best for
you. You make a complete fool of me. Now this. It's disgusting.
I'm not standing for it. You can get out.'

He called to the cat, who was curled up with us, but it
wouldn't move.

'It's all my fault,' said Denise, crying. Howard was looking at
her in unrestrained horror. So was I.

'Can I use the phone?' I asked.

'No you can't. Get out!'

'I'm allowed one call by law.'

'Just one then. You make me sick to my stomach.'

My one call drew a blank. I checked my case at Penn Station,
had a wash, and took out my address book. Under 'Ambulance'
it had 'Omar, florist, room to let'.

They Look All Right If You've Had a Drink

Omar had known I would call, he said. He'd been to the Gypsy
Caravan and Margot had told him a man would come from
Europe to aid him with his work.

'I thought you were a florist,' I said.

'Ah yes, but I write poetry,' said Omar.

'How can I help you?'

'I lack acceptance in London, you see.'

'I see.'

'Look, I have a wedding right now. You wanna go along?'

'I'd love to.'

'I work in conjunction with two other firms,' Omar explained as we got into his van marked 'Nijinsky Floral Tributes and Occasions'. 'Each one collects the other's used decorations from the venue and resells it to his own customer. We carry on like that until the material is unusable.'

'Do you charge for collection?'

'We're working on it.'

'I don't think literary London should present you with any problems.'

'You really think so?'

'I think you're a natural.'

The Far-Out Cactus and Foliage Company were supplying sweet peas to a Bar Mitzvah in Brooklyn. We hi-jacked a hundred baskets of the silly things, hurled them into the van and raced them round to a wedding reception in Queens.

'Smarten up, you little buggers,' hissed Omar, as we commenced unloading. 'Sweet peas are good for this kind of work,' he told me. 'They give a blurred effect which makes it hard to say what stage they're currently at.'

'Are these ones dead yet?'

'Of course,' he said, doing something vicious to them with a pocket aerosol.

'I suppose they look all right if you've had a drink,' I said.

'Exactly,' said Omar. 'That's the whole philosophy.'

Everyone at the reception was overjoyed with the effect created by Omar's flowers. They gave us a bottle of champagne to drink and they added some money to Omar's cheque. Then Omar made a date with one of the ushers for later that night and we prepared to leave.

'What time shall I arrange for the flowers to be disposed of, madam?' enquired Omar in his best undertaker's manner.

'Six would be fine. Are you sure it isn't too much trouble?'

'Nothing is too much trouble, madam.'

Omar phoned The Blushing Flower Service to tell them where to collect and his day's work was done.

Shaving Back to Happiness

Neither resident nor tourist, I have an uneasy status in this town. I have a kind of routine, and yet I am also about to leave.

It's my second last Saturday. Why aren't I out there? I think of all the brains in all the buildings, telling their tired bodies to smarten up and live. After all, isn't this the moment they've been waiting for? The reason so many New Yorkers live alone, hoarding their nerves for the night-time? Like plants or insects they find what they passionately need by an invisible communication across the city. They come home from work and they go to bed for five hours – alone. Then they get up and go.

> Whoever you are, go out into the evening,
> Leaving your room of which you know each bit,
> Your house is the last before the infinite,
> Whoever you are.
> — Rilke, 'Initiation'.

Nine o'clock. A million futures hang back a few moments more. In mirrors, eyes glance into eyes that will later pierce the gloom of bars in search of other eyes, other glances. Ties are being chosen. I love this lonely dressing for the fray. I shave myself back to a boy, then I shake out my black jeans and put them on again, fill my medicine bottle with gin. I haven't washed my hair for a few days and it stands up like an actor's. I've noticed myself becoming slightly more exaggerated in the last few weeks. New York is a course in self-knowledge for the prematurely tidy, the artificially humble. It isn't like London, anyway, where you can shave as close as you like and still come home alone.

Tonight There'll Be . . .

When you first enter a room full of people the girls are always beautiful and you too are powerful. You have newness and no past. You have luck on your side still, having not yet touched your share of it. If you speak to a girl now, she will be beautiful, because her beauty is in proportion to your courage. It lasts about a quarter of an hour. After that you can forget it. Ugliness and old age set in. Time yawns and luck leaves without you. Those same pretty girls that were there when you came in have disappeared, or were never there in the first place, or else you have left it too late to follow them. Somebody must possess them, you think, consoling yourself with the obvious, but what does it matter so long as it isn't you? Being in the right place at the right time isn't enough for a man. You have to speak! It's one of those things.

Beauty is courage, you realise, and courage is beauty. *That* is all you need to know . . .

. . . *No Hesitating*

'Thanks,' I thought, as I got out of the taxi, 'I'll try and remember that.'

The party was in four knocked-through apartments overlooking the East River — 'The boys next door had their number done in neon for the sailors . . .' — names and semi-names, literary and not so literary, live-ins, live-outs and other acknowledgments moved with their drinks against the majestic backdrop. I passed among the attractive crowd at that perfect stage of drunkenness when the whole world is like water off a duck's back.

It lasted until a familiar London face forced itself, contorting, into my view.

'Jenny, what are you doing here?' I asked. 'Where's Frank?'

'Frank and I finally split up.'

'Wonderful. I never could stand him. Where are you living?'

'I'm living at home. For the time being. You know.'

'You've moved downstairs or what?'

'I haven't got round to it yet.'

'You mean you still sleep . . .'

'Well, it's difficult. There's only one bed . . .'

'But you don't . . .'

'Only when *I* feel like it.'

'Anyway, you're on your own in New York are you?'

'As a matter of fact Frank's over there. He's been so sweet about it all. Frank . . .'

Frank and Jenny linked arms and smiled at me happily. Goodbye Jenny and Frank.

'What I like about writing,' someone was saying, 'is that you don't have to show your worksheets to anyone . . .'

'Unlike surgeons, I suppose . . .'

'Or generals . . .'

'I thought those *were* your worksheets, Ted.'

'It's a coward's game if you ask me.'

'I had an insight about that . . .'

'I would very much like to sleep with you one night.'

'I know, Jimmy. But what can you offer me in return?'

'I have these tickets for this play . . . I don't know . . .'

The gorgeous red-headed literary agent said she was looking for non-fiction manuscripts and I found myself telling her I was doing an 'impressions of America'. (The first I had heard of it.)

'What's the peg?' She wanted to know.

'Interviews with nonentities.'

'Have your read Studs Terkel?'

'No.'

'That's interviews with nonentities. Studs is the best interviewer in America. He did prostitutes, tramps, thieves. It turned out their lives were incredibly dramatic . . .'

If she didn't want impressions of America, how about a biography of Neal Cassidy? There was one.

Anne Winchester was a striking English girl who had written a musical which everyone said was BIG. We got on well for a few minutes, then I realised it was time to meet Omar at the theatre. He'd given me a ticket to a play by a friend of his. On the way out I bumped into two perfect little teenagers with eyes like pieces of barbed wire. I reached the street and went back. The teenagers were nowhere to be seen, but Frank was there.

'I thought you left,' he said. 'What did you come back for?'

'I wondered if you 'n Jenny would like lunch tomorrow,' I whimpered.

'Love to,' crowed Frank 'n Jenny.

Take My Advice and Burn All Your Plays

The taxi to the theatre entered Cental Park twice. The trip cost a king's ransom. At the box office was a message from Omar saying he couldn't make it. A girl took my ticket and showed me directly on to a tiny stage where some acting was already going on. I looked at her in confusion and she pointed to a sign, SIT ON BLACK AREAS ONLY PLEASE. I sat down on a small black area almost between some actor's black-booted legs.

'Why don't you make yourself comfortable,' said this man sarcastically, breaking off his speech to address me.

'I can't,' I said. 'There's nothing to lean against.'

'Sit over here,' said a kindly peasant woman.

'Thanks,' I said, moving over next to her.

'Stay where you are now,' said the actor.

The play seemed to be about Tolstoy as a young man and an old man, with special reference to Today. The audience were supposed to be Tolstoy's household and serfs. I tried to enjoy it, but I found myself wishing I was back at the party with the two teenagers and Anne Winchester. I wondered if an audience was allowed to go home if it found itself outnumbered by the actors. I stuck it for half an hour, then I got to my feet.

'Where do you think *you're* going?' said the actor in boots, who was Tolstoy.

'Back to the party,' I said.

'Get back to your place.'

'No.'

When I got there Anne Winchester was leaving. The party was over, she said. I made her come back inside with me and she hunted me up a drink. I told her about Tolstoy and she said she had to see it. We taxied there and crept conspicuously on to the peculiar set.

'Sit on the black areas,' I whispered to Anne.

'What the fuck you think you're doing walking in and out of here all the time?' bellowed Tolstoy.

'I brought someone from the party,' I said. 'She had to see it.'

'I'll speak to *you* afterwards.'

At the end of the play Chekhov came to visit Tolstoy on his railway station deathbed.

'Take my advice,' said Tolstoy, pulling his beard. 'You must burn all your plays.'

Chekhov pulled his own beard a couple of times and seemed in two minds about this. When the lights came up the 'audience' found themselves alone on the stage.

'Let's get out of here before Tolstoy comes back,' I said.

'Jesus God Almighty!' said Anne.

Press Button to Hold Desired Symbol

Chips of green perspex, their edges illuminated as if from nowhere, represented the sprigs of verdure round the plaster roots of the obligatory gay-world palm tree in the lobby of the luxury Public Relations apartment on Park Avenue where I met Vicky.

A divorce-party-cum-going-away-sale was in progress. The prematurely tanned owner of the apartment told me she was chucking her job, husband and apartment and marrying someone older, richer and more powerful, called Judas, in Miami. She told a man to get me a drink.

American cocktails are triple-thick and these were quadruples, to muffle the outlandish prices she was asking for the pyramids of redundant props and paraphernalia that had failed to hold together her Public Relations marriage to a friend of one of Norman Mailer's agents. Norman Mailer was there, she said, and Truman Capote of course. You couldn't see them, but they were there, or on their way, or their agents were there, or had promised to be there. So naturally we were there too, and bidding like mad for all this stuff that was squeezing us against the walls. A video of Bob Dylan singing 'Idiot Wind' had been left on, with '$1,000' painted across the screen. The tabby cat was going for free, being pregnant the naughty girl. The mink coats cost a little more. After a moment's astute questioning my hostess took my elbow and introduced me to a big box of LPs, saying they were only 50c each, which was fair, I thought.

I started going through these alongside a skinny girl in a shift who was talking to me before I met her and was still talking when I saw the last of her several months later. She seemed to be telling me about her uncle who had been a sideman for Jack Teagarden. This man had led a fantastic life, mostly in France and Scandinavia, where he had died owing thousands. She was flipping through the records at such a pace by now that I gave up and let her talk. We whipped past a ten-inch LP of Eddy Duchin playing Cole Porter and this girl went off into a haze of stories about a boyfriend of hers who used to smoke grass out of a rifle in Vietnam, until he was lost out there. He'd written a song to her. He wasn't good-looking, but he could go two days without a wink of sleep. I asked how many days she could go without drawing breath and she stopped talking for a moment to look at me, her large, attractive mouth still open. I thought she was going to say 'I'm hungry,' but she said:

'I'm Vicky.' It was as if she had snapped the handcuffs on. We left the records and moved to where the drinks and drugs offered displacement activity.

Large heaps of marijuana straight from the fields lay on every flat surface, as if someone has just mowed the lawn. Everyone was talking at once as if their lives depended on it. You don't make sense in New York, you make yourself felt, and you don't wait for someone to stop talking, you butt in and stay there: film stories, promotional gimmicks, nutcase histories, suicide attempts (comic), break-ins, break-outs, second-hand mugging reports, chat-show foul-ups, and the occasional slightly hysterical story of some ex-friend's pathetic failure to cut the candle in the Great Making-It Stakes, his reduced circumstances, his increased impotence, his subsequent divorce, his children's comments, his own lies, his suicide attempt on holiday with some kind friends of someone on a farm where they slaughter minks, too weird, but there you are. Gay, gay, gay, with every now and then a quickie travel sketch on a subject of interest to everyone: America! How someone went to a ranch, you know, with cowboys? How someone else had, with a series of little shrieks, discovered the Prairies, and it was just like *High Noon.* I noticed how America was being perceived by these Manhattanites as a medium of Entertainment, a kind of sub-genre of the Hollywood Musical. Pretty soon the whole country was aglow with the highlights of a tv commercial.

'We broke in two really wild bronco stallions . . .' (a wiry blonde).

'We butchered all our own meat for a month . . .' (a young publisher).

'I sat in with the original Storyville jazz band,' (an enthusiast).

'Bill and I were married on the spur of the moment in this little round village church surrounded by corn. It was like *Oklahoma.*'

'Honey it *was* Oklahoma.'

But Vicky was different. She had excitable headlights for eyes. And I loved the way she talked. She would launch into a topic like walking on to a stage, gathering ears with her eyes, clearly not the slightest notion of what she was going to say next, but fraily dominant still and never at a loss. What's more, it was all done at least partly for my benefit and I was fascinated by her. She kept glancing at me and showing me her magnificent teeth. She had something to show me at home, she said, so we found our way to a taxi.

What She Showed Me at Home

Vicky's bed was on a shelf up near the ceiling of a smart open-plan studio. I took one look at that high plateau, shrouded in mist, and could see straight away that once you got up there it would be difficult to turn back.

'You're not my ideal,' Vicky said, 'but you'll do for intercession.' Intercession being half-term. She was doing American Literature, she said, showing me a letter from Ernest Hemingway to her husband. I read the letter, which was some boring point about sport. Then I asked about her husband. The man was an absolute charmer apparently, a handsome and witty stud with an ever-burning desire for her body, a heroin-addict and bisexual thief.

'Yeah, we had an amphetamine honeymoon Zak and I. One horny old beatnik and his child bride. He was erect for a month.'

'What happened to him?'

'He wilted! He drifted west I think, then he went to prison of course.'

Before long Vicky and I were sprawling on an uncomfortable couch, boasting and necking alternately. Every now and then she would disengage herself and run around looking for a signed copy of some book or other. She seemed to have slept with every author on her course. One exotic lover after the previous world famous admirer was paraded for my amazement, adding feather after feather to Vicky's imaginary plumage.

She would lean towards me with her sharp teeth showing and interrupt everything I thought of myself, her huge bright eyes alight with some fatal fever for celebrity. Every time I tried to get on top of her, William Styron or someone would come between us. Even death seemed to pose no barrier to her intimate knowledge of a man. Was it a test? Or had she got me round here just to have a nice row?

The excitement of being horizontally entwined with Vicky slowly ebbed, due to constant interruptions from the great. I stifled my disbelief and tried to stay awake. As dawn came up I must have dozed because I woke to find bits of Vicky's clothes coming away in my hands as if they had rotted with the great time we had lain there. But by then it was too late.

She was still talking, naturally, but now Marvin was there too, her flatmate, and she was addressing her discourse to him. He was trying to get to work, but she made him listen to a story about herself and Otto Preminger, shouting through to him in the kitchen while he made us coffee.

'I'm not a good lay,' she told me later. 'I only look like one.'

The large print giveth, the small print taketh away.

Zak Phones

We woke that evening to find ourselves still on the day bed, exhausted, dirty and cross.

'When are we going?' asked Vicky.

'Going where?'

'New Orleans.'

'New Orleans? Did I say that? I thought you had to go to school.'

'Yes you did. So what if I do? I thought we were going for intercession. You said'. . .'

'No, that was your idea. I meant next month, if I could get a car. I have these readings to do first.'

'Well isn't that great? That's wonderful news. So we're not going, right?'

'Right.'

'Zak phoned while you were asleep you know. All the way from the coast.'

'Which coast?'

'There's only one coast, baby. The Coast coast. The Barbary Coast. The West Coast. He said he'd come over for intercession if I liked. I said, no, I was going to New Orleans. I'd met this guy who wanted to take me. Zak said that was cool, he wouldn't come this time. Now I'll miss him.'

'Call him back.'

'You wanna pay for the call?'

'Sure.'

She scales the perilous fire-escape to her sulky sleeping area in the clouds. I'm just getting ready to go when Marvin enters.

'Hi Marvin honey child. Got any bread for me today?'

'No. Sorry.' Marvin nods to himself like mad.

'Oh Marv, like you to meet, uh, like you to . . .' (peels of laughter) 'What did you say your name was again?'

'Hugo, what's yours?'

'Marvin, that used to be Hugo.'

3
THE POETRY READING TOUR

The Last of the Patriots

The railroad follows the Hudson river north. The glare of industry stings your eyes. Sidings and sheds and smoking chimneys. Hardware scattered haphazardly beside the river as if a bad child has left his things out to rust. A refuse skip labelled 'Monument Valley' trundles by. A freight wagon contains 'Liquid Flo-Sweet – Sugar For Industry'. Here's a place called 'Auto-Wreck'.

Hazy cliffs rise majestically on the far shore. I can almost make out the line of Indians, their arms folded, looking through half-closed eyes at this Guernica-scape. A partially sunken speed boat has a luminous orange buoy attached to it. Near by stands Roxy's Lighthouse. At Greystone there's a vicious white dust in the air and motionless old men with faces like clowns where they have licked their lips clean of the powder. The words 'Shock Control' are dragged slowly across my vision.

Now we're at Albany. The little white HMV dog squats on the tallest building, his ear cocked crazily to the wind. Giant letters exhort me to 'THINK ABOUT THE AMERICAN FLAG'.

'In case you got nothing better to, this here is the Mohawk Valley we're entering . . .' I looked round and there was the ticket collector, a Dickensian figure with waxed moustaches, addressing us from the back of the carriage. 'If you care to look out of the left hand window, we're just about to pass the first stone

43

house to be built in the valley. It was built by Sir William Johnston from England for his daughter in 1794. There it is now.' And he passed on to the next carriage.

'He was in the papers not long ago,' said my neighbour. 'They were doing a series on the last of the patriots.'

Nowhere Like Toronto

The man ahead of me at the Canadian Customs looked very reluctant to say out loud what he did for a living. 'Import clothes from Guatemala,' I heard him whisper. The officials looked dubious about this, so the man made up something about having a ring for his girl in Toronto. No one believed this Yank, but they let him go. My own cultural mission was looked on much more favourably by the upstanding frontier guard. 'Reading poetry, eh? Your own or other people's?'

A table was laid for twenty in a room off the main hall at York College, Toronto. I stood drinking with the chaplain, waiting for the special guests to arrive and identifying with the prawn cocktails waiting pinkly for the faculty jaws. Only half of them turned up however, as Marshall McLuhan had chosen this moment to come home and was holding out his death-of-the-word tidings elsewhere on campus. We bunched together at the top of the table, commiserating in whispers about the Canadian Cultural Wilderness. Those not of the cloth seemed either Irish or Scottish, anxious only to be reassured once more that they had done the right thing in seeking a new life for themselves in this essentially decent country. A short silence in the right place would have had them groping for their passports.

The reading was hardly the joyous affirmation of life my audience had been hoping for. I thought it was, but then I like poems on impotence and death. In fact, I was more than usually aware of the incongruity between the 'subjects' of my poems and my apparent adventurousness in travelling so far to read them to such a tiny audience till then ignorant of my existence. I was a walking contradiction and it was this I left hanging in the air after every reading. 'The age of writing has passed,' goes the Marshall McLuhan nag. 'We must invent a NEW METAPHOR.' Yes, talking about it.

After the reading I expressed some enthusiasm for seeing the city. At Grossman's there was a blues group, but you have to sit

44

down for music in Canada and there weren't any tables. One of our group said, by way of explanation, that you're a nobody in Canada if you have on a narrow tie, meaning me in my sixties stuff. Then we passed a tower which I think he said was the tallest edifice in the free-standing world and I was to put my head on the back shelf of the car in order better to appreciate this monstrosity. I said I'd take his word for it and an awkward silence fell over us as we drove down on through those purged and passionless streets.

'May I have all your receipts please,' said the secretary when I went to hunt up my cheque from Finance the next morning.

'I don't think I'm on expenses,' I explained.

'You don't understand,' she said. 'We need your receipts in order to pay you your fee. Your fare, meals etc.'

'I don't keep receipts for that kind of thing.'

'Well, I don't know what Accounts will say,' she said, realising sadly that she'd have to give me the money anyway.

An Interlude of Unsurpassed Excitement

Niagara Falls is a traditional honeymoon attraction. Newlyweds find it encouraging to board the *Maid of the Mist* and to view from close up a hundred thousand tons of foam crashing every second over an eighty foot precipice. As my Benares guide told me in the 'Nepalese Love Temple', 'It put idea of generation into mind of man.' The Canadian Tourist Board is more discreet:

> The Great Gorge Trip is an exciting and romantic experience in intimate contact with Nature's handiwork at the very edge of the awesome Whirlpool Rapids. Man and Nature come together with an unforgettable experience of sight and sound. The scenic tunnel is truly an interlude of unsurpassed excitement. Here Man has used his utmost skill and native artistry to coax from Nature new miracles of artistry and colour.

We read that the Niagara Plaza has 'the Big Look' in Observation Towers. 'The Tower Ride is the beginning of an unforgettable experience.' While for those of a more studious outlook 'Britain's Historical Past is portrayed in our London Wax Museum.' (Closed, naturally.)

Waxworks proliferate, including numerous renderings of the highly Freudian 'Houdini', who used to go over the Falls in milk churns, and Blondin, who walked across on a rope, cooked and ate his breakfast in mid-stream and once offered to convey the Prince of Wales to America on his shoulders. The Prince declined, claiming that his rank obliged him to stay on terra firma. 'See his personal lock collection', ran the brochure for the Houdini Museum:

> Learn the art of sleeping under water and spontaneous combustion. Stop a speeding bullet. Enter the escapist's period living room and see your own body disappear into thin air. Lose your loved ones in the Black Hole of Calcutta (Adults Only). Be mystified by our resident Magician. Continuous Performances.

When I got there the resident Magician was seeking his fortune elsewhere, but the redoubtable Houdini's instruments of restriction and bondage were laid out under greenish spotlights, shrivelled and ashamed-looking. Poor Houdini. He died a broken man. Not broken by Niagara or his battered milk churn, but by the march of progress. Aeroplanes and electricity, radio and moving pictures had upstaged his good faith. He was an anachronism, escaping out of nowhere into nothingness.

Off the Rails

On the train back to New York, more and more schoolboy alarm at the three-month term stretching unpredictably ahead of me like a plot I have to get right before I can go home again. Or is it just the thought of tonight's probable bedlessness? Travel is really a test of the imagination. Homesickness its failure. So this kind of depression is just a failure to get up and see what's happening in the snack bar.

I get up. In the bar are six black boys with long-handled metal combs dug into the backs of their heads like tomahawks. They wobble their legs and bow, pour drink everywhere, slap hands and shout, spin round and stare at my woebegone countenance, suppressing their laughter. Maybe I'll stay on this train down to Washington, then get the bus to South Carolina from there. That'll solve the night for me. I had just thought of that when there was a grinding crash and the train came off the rails. One of the blacks fell over in mid-laugh, then burst out laughing again. Luckily the train was just entering Penn Station, New York, so we were going very slowly. I looked out of the window and saw wheels embedded in cinders. Forlorn porters were staring at us incredulously. The black boys leant out of the window and sang 'We're making trains worth traveling again,' Amtrak's desperate rallying cry.

No Sleeping in Penn Station

It was ten o'clock. The next train to Washington was at 4.15. I phoned Vicky, but there was no answer. I lay down on a bench and tried to sleep. There was an explosion in my dream as a policeman's nightstick struck the bench near my head. No sleeping. Wake up now. Where you heading? What time's your train? Somehow I remembered where I was. '4.15 to Washington.' I sat there watching a foul-mouthed old woman being thrown out of the women's toilets three times before being led away. Then the cleaners arrived with Hoovers like phantom dune buggies, the flexes plugged into points underfoot and vast areas of the hall roped off at a time. A camp young man sat down beside me and asked where I was going. When I told him he said he would come to Washington with me. Did I want to score some uppers or grass or go to the rest room with him? He took out his wallet and showed me a photograph of New Orleans. There was a horror comic stuck in his belt. I said, 'After Washington, it's Alaska. We could meet there.' 'Oh no, man, that's too cold. I'm from New Orleans and I ain't never going back there.' 'I wasn't serious.' 'No, but I am, man.' He went off and offered himself to some anoraked itinerant. I watched the Buchenwald-faced night cop toying sadistically with his nightstick like some hallucinatory drag drum majorette. With the thong round his wrist he would let the truncheon cartwheel downwards, hitting the floor with a 'clack', then ricocheting smartly back into his open hand. He swung one leg forward from the hip and began to strut in the direction of the young queer. A poor paranoid black woman was kicking thin air and screeching abuse at a wall. She too had to go.

What Is Black and White and Loveable to See

I wanted to sleep on the train, but a very old man sat down next to me and began overflowing with information in the New York way. Did I know he'd been to London when he was young? He couldn't remember which year exactly, but it was before the crash. He'd stayed in London and had met someone in the perfume business who had been a real gentleman. He himself was in the carton and container racket. Or had been before his son moved West. I wondered how and where he'd slept with his first woman, but remained silent. It was still dark, my face thinner in the window: Washington at last. I bought a postcard with these laudible sentiments:

> What is black and white and loveable to see
> Are the new pandas of Washington D.C.
> Given by the State Department to the public
> This gift was from the Chinese People's Republic
>
> The pandas are of God's creation so fine
> A great symbol of the love from the divine
> Both Hsing and Ling are at the Washington Zoo
> Living and waiting for a visit from you.

Rows of tv chairs in the Washington Greyhound Bus Station. On each the inscription which has branded itself on my brain: 'Chair for TV Viewing "Please" ', and underneath it: 'Made in Salt Lake City'. I put in my quarter and watched the middle fifteen minutes of a comedy about a man and woman who daren't make love because their children are holding an important business dinner downstairs. The wife runs down in her undies and the mayor leaves in a huff. Then the screen went blank and I read: 'Chair for TV Viewing "Please" '.

The Anthologist's Approach

'My name is Houdini,' I began, reading to the small audience from the brochure I had picked up at Niagara Falls:

> I would like to show you my personal collection of locks, keys, handcuffs and straitjackets. Later tonight I shall reveal to you the secrets of the world's greatest illusions in

magic, including my walking through a brick wall, split personality and dead man's noose. Don't be afraid to ask to see the original 'Decapitation' and 'Cremation' scenes, my glass box and battered milk churn . . .

My words echoed back and forth among the sausage-shaped acoustical baffles of the Great Hall, Charlotte University, North Carolina. When they came to roost, there was an eerie silence which later turned out to have been the highspot of the show. How was I going to get out of this one? As usual I went over the falls in my battered milk churn. The audience had seen it all before.

After the reading there was a party for me in the college nightclub. Dozens of new people appeared and made straight for the chocolate brownies spaced out like goat droppings on long trestle tables. For a while I was surrounded by munching academics who had just been to a religious discussion given by Jack Anderson, gossip-columnist of the *Washington Post*. Had I been myself, by any chance? Did I play golf or just jog? I talked to one glazed professor called Druid Wakowski who had a bundle of hand-calligraphed magazines for sale. Some of them had gold leaf on them, he told me, opening his eyes very wide. What did I think of the poetry of Clayton Eshelmann? 'Just a *tremendous* poet,' he said. I expressed interest in this and asked the name of one of Eshelmann's books.

'They're all essential reading for any, er, student,' said Druid.

'I know, but tell me one poem you liked, so I can . . .'

'Oh, I don't know about that. Taken as a whole, you see. His *total* output. Just a tremendous *poet* . . .'

'No, but fling out the name of just *one* poem so I'll be able to understand what you meant.'

'For God's sake,' said Druid. 'I can't . . . I mean, what's this *anthologist's* approach to literature?'

I noticed that the brownies and myself were not the only attraction in the club. In a corner was a hunched figure strumming morosely on a guitar. This was the poet Crock Hennessey. Crock seemed indifferent to his surroundings, but it wasn't long before groups of academics were detaching themselves from the trestle tables and forming a half-circle round Crock and his guitar, which I noticed was increasing in volume. I soon found myself loitering redundantly on the outskirts of this crowd. For something to do, I began nibbling one of the remaining brownies. Crock had out-manoeuvred me. By now he was opening up his bull-like throat for 'The Blue-Tail Fly'.

Trapper, Woodsman and Public Relations Executive

Crock Hennessey is a big man, cast in the Hemingway mould; according to his best-selling *Hennessey Eats Out*, a former star college boxer, night bomber pilot with more than a hundred missions in World War Two, trapper, woodsman and Public Relations Executive.

'Take a look at this,' he said, handing me a steel archer's bow as I arrived at his lakeside ranch the next day. 'Try and draw it.'

I laid hold on the wire, but couldn't budge it.

'Like this,' he said, drawing it back with ease. 'This'll out-shoot a Winchester. Pierce an inch of solid steel.' He gave me a bear hug. 'Come with me,' he said. 'I want to show you something.' He led the way through the house. As we passed his wife she put strong drinks into our hands without a word or a look. Holding these, we strode towards the lake. I had only an hour before my bus to Charlottesville, Virginia, and Crock had a lot he wanted to show me, he said.

The first thing he showed me was America.

'See?' he said, sweeping the impressive horizon with his arm. 'It's big. It's beautiful. That's America. America's big. I'm big. Milton was big. Shakespeare was big. And you know something?' His mighty arm went round my shoulder, 'No cock-sucking fag of an English critic ain't gonna tell me no different. But come back to the house. I got a few things I want to show you back there.'

As we entered the house, his wife refilled our glasses from a bottle of Wild Turkey.

'Take a look at that,' said Crock, pointing past her to what may have been the head of a gnu or caribou. 'Killed it with my knife.'

'Did you mount it yourself?' I asked.

'Nah. Don't have time for that kind of thing,' he said, making a face as if taxidermy was an occupation for cock-sucking English critics. 'Listen to this.' He strode to the tape deck and banged on some Blue Grass music. 'That's me on guitar.'

We listened to the music for thirty seconds, then Crock appeared to lose patience with it. He banged it off again.

'Seen this?' he asked.

In a wall cabinet hung a human scalp. I thought he was going to tell me that it belonged to the fag English critic, but it turned out he had won it arm-wrestling in Alaska.

'You arm-wrassle?' he asked.

'Never,' I said eagerly.

His wife put another glass of Wild Turkey into his out-stretched hand. He gave me a bear hug.

'Come here,' he said. 'I want to show you something.'

We went into another room where Crock's many published works were laid out on a table.

'See?' he said. 'Books. Good ones. Plenty of 'em. All of 'em by me. You want one? Have one.'

He picked up a book and wrote 'At the beginning,' in it for me. Another bear hug and it was time for me to leave. 'It's been good,' he said, tears streaming down his face. The last I saw of him he was slumped on the gatepost in despair.

Williams, Younger, More Anxious

'A brief gathering beforehand', ran the article in the *Charlottes-ville News*, 'found Galway Kinnell heavy on the hors d'oeuvres, beer in hand, relaxing after a tennis match and still organising the programme for his third reading in two days. Williams, younger, more anxious, clutched a stronger drink and con-versed congenially, yet quite intensely with those who approached him.' Clutching, anxious and intense. Thanks, Barbara. But what happened to 'debonair' and 'handsome'? She moves on to the reading: 'When Galway Kinnell came into the analytical glare of the Chemistry Auditorium it was like a lumberjack replacing a songbird.'

Readings make me squirm. It's because every poem ever written falls short of 'poetry'. Yet it is Poetry a reading tries to celebrate.

'This one will gross you out,' said Kinnell, introducing his poem 'The Bear'.

When it was over Irvin Ehrenpreis, my host, came up and asked me to come to his poetry class the next morning. 'Was I that bad?' I asked.

Later I met Louise Gluck, poet in residence at Charlottes-ville, or rather just outside it. The delegates hadn't known about her child when they appointed her and instead of putting her in the usual quarters had swept her to the outskirts in a fit of institutional propriety.

She lived without a car in the ugly and inconvenient Mimosa Drive. Students came in relays of cars to her classes, but her life was unwieldy with babysitters and taxis. Virginia is very much Old South and the colour of a woman's skin turns black very quickly if conventions are disturbed. She seemed lonely, ex-hausted, caught in a crossfire. Half-joking, I asked if she'd seen the cover of the current *National Lampoon* which had a picture of the Virgin Mary being thrown out of her home for being preg-nant. She didn't respond.

No Time at Bowling Green

'Where you heading?' said a voice at my elbow. An old woman was moving up the bench towards me. Bus stations are like chessboards. If you don't keep an eye on your diagonals you're liable to get checked. Your opponent opens with a question which can't have the answer 'No'. 'No' is where they live and they want to get out of there.

'Where you heading?'

'North.'

'I'm heading north. I've been travelling for a month. You wanna see the map? My cousins live in Lake Charles. They needed the room. They said I'd set fire to the house with my newspapers. But I like to keep up with what's happening, don't you? Of course, I had to leave them behind when I left Lake Charles. But I can sleep on the buses. I've been on the road a month and only one night in a motel . . .' She tucked some grey hair back under a kind of bed-cap.

'If you look after God, he'll look after you,' she told me, as she found half an apple in her plastic bag bulging with newspapers. 'I'm gonna meet a reverend gentleman in Idaho. You want I should write you from there? You Jewish? No, I can see you're a nice boy . . .'

'All aboard now. And thanks for going Greyhound.' It's the fuel crisis and posters along the way show two smiling men – one white, one black – sitting in the front seat of a car, the white man driving. Another says 'Don't be Fuelish!' with a picture of a boy switching something off – downwards of course in the States. There's a 'Drug Fair' and a sign in a bush says 'Our Lady of Angels'. This is Stamford, Virginia. Or rather 'Stiamford'. In Woodbridge there's a Buffeteria with 'hot coffee brewin'. There are bright yellow fire engines in this part of the world. It's started to look like the storybooks, with little shacks like old shoes in among the cheap brush and winter trees. Much 'Realty' up for grabs. Random weatherboard dolls' houses in Dumfries are painted pale pink and green, the vagrant grass between them parched, appearing summery already. No fences anywhere, American style. Just houses on the land or built on stilts with mosquito-wired stoops.

Behind me on the bus a young man is giving his girlfriend a terrible ear-bashing. He has a hectoring, told-you-so Southern self-righteousness with which he lays down the laws of history. 'After every war there's a depression,' he observes. No matter what she says he repeats his last remark. 'After every war there's a depression.' He's just admitted he was born in 1951, now he's telling her England was conquered by Hitler. She tries to check him but he goes right on: 'Yeah, the English were conquered by Hitler all right.' I imagine he must be some big handsome lad to be so confident, but when I turn round he's a little squirt in specs. What's surprising is they're both black.

'This Coach is Rest Room Equipped.' Yes, it is, but it's not restful keeping your balance in there in the chromium-plated dark. So I wait for the bus to stop again. A kid with a broken neck gets on. Are we going to Quantico? 'No, straight over.' This is Prince William County, where mobile homes grow like mushrooms. Chaplinesque prefabs litter the woods near Stafford. Things a shade run down. A pit full of old cars is probably some old character's livelihood, with a case of rattlers 'in back'. Now here's a big muddy river of forested islands at shacky Fredericksburg. 'White Rock Cream Soda' sounds tempting, but you can't risk getting down when it's 'No time at Bowling Green' or somewhere.

No Oil Painting

I had a window seat and I dozed. I had just woken up and was thinking what a daft name 'Putt-Putt' was for 'America's Quality Golf Courses' when I felt a hand on my knee. I snapped round and saw that someone was offering me a bottle of whisky. 'Have a drink,' he ordered. He looked dangerous, one of those re-hash jobs with the hairline pulled down over the stitches, the raw nerve-ends covered with a kind of suit from the waxworks: collar, tie and jacket too flat-looking. I should have known better. If you get on a Greyhound early and get your window seat, you're a sitting duck for the company-mongering speed-freaks and queers who make up the staple diet of these vora-cious intestines for digesting human beings and their woes. The trick is to take your place in the queue late. By the time you get on, the window seats are gone. So you walk slowly down the aisle, your eyes relaxed but vigilant, weighing the odds of progressing towards the back or settling for this cowboy here who seems to be nodding off already.

This time I was cornered. 'Have a drink,' he told me again. The Scotch was Dewar's. 'I was buried in de wars,' he said. 'I never came home. You see that?' He lifted an index finger like a blasted oak. I waited to hear what he had done with this gross digit, but he didn't pursue the matter. Soon the whisky had engaged my own sleepy imagination and I was going in for the uniquely inti-mate confidences which seem to flow from one's lips when one is crushed elbow to elbow in these flying confessionals.

'Say, you're English aren't you?' he asked. That was all I needed. I gave him a ten-thousand word biography of myself and before I had finished I realised I had made yet another life-friend, prepared to follow me to the ends of Virginia should I so desire him. He had nowhere particular to go himself, he told me. He had thought of visiting a certain ex-jailer friend of his in Newport News, but that could wait. 'We got to know one another inside,' he told me, adding alarmingly: 'but he was no oil painting.'

By now we were hitting the outskirts of Williamsburg and Johnny was gathering up his packages in readiness to accom-pany me to the poetry reading. 'It'd be a gas,' he told me youthfully, drawing in his belt. 'Get pissed – I've heard about Williamsburg. That's the old-time colonial town ain't it? That why you visiting there?'

'No, no, not at all. I was just invited by the college.'

'Poetry! I used to write poetry. The Ballad of the Reading Gaol. Have a drop for the road?'

'No thanks. I'm being met by some professor. I won't be able to stay with you any more. It's been great talking to you – and thanks for the drinks – that's really set me up. I'm not looking forward to this.'

'Don't do it then. Screw them professor fellas. I'll go along with you. Say I'm your manager. I could manage you. Have a few drinks. I'll read a poem myself . . .' Here he rolled up his sleeve and showed me a great scar where he'd had a tattoo removed.

'What was it before?' I asked.

'That would be telling now, wouldn't it,' he said, still making as if to accompany me. I said goodbye and scrambled for the door. He wasn't looking when I waved to him.

Buried in de Wars

I was combing my hair in a mirror in the bus station, when I saw Johnny arguing with a soldier on the other side of the hall. So he'd got down here after all. Did he mean to stay? I prayed it wasn't on my behalf he'd decided to visit Williamsburg.

Just then a naval captain approached me. This was Doctor K. He took off his yachting cap and said he would take me straight to Hospitality House, a vast mock-tudor motel, 'the gift of an Old Boy in oil. But it's nearly always empty.' In the lobby a real-unreal fire 'blazed' disconcertingly beside a life-size replica of a vintage Le Mans racing car. Richly carpeted corridors led to a cavernous chamber where I was to change and wash and be ready within an hour.

There was ice in the bathroom and a colour telly at the foot of the bed. I put the telly on to keep me awake and went into a trance in front of an afternoon panel game in which three married couples competed against each other for some heavily promoted junk consumerables, such as automobile hooverettes and inflatable drinks trays for the pool. The panel-master was describing a situation for them: 'You're driving along with your wife,' he enthused, 'you're going through this elegant suburb. You notice all the trashcans are out. Suddenly you see this antique figurine sticking out of one of the trashcans. You stop the car, but which one of you jumps out to get the figurine, you or your wife?' The couples were then separated, like hogs prior to servicing, and each one asked what he/she thought would happen.

The house phone rang and it was Doctor K. come to collect me. This time he wore a Tyrolean jacket and perky green hat with a porcupine cockade in the side of it. He'd left off the Lederhosen. He told me his uncle used to make musical instruments for 'Pound 'n Yeats'.

We drove to the Cascades Restaurant for a delicious dinner and by the time I got to the reading I was too drunk to speak. I went down some winding stairs to a gents which had special handles for cripples. I hung on to these and read: 'I was once, a long time ago, a hippie in the best suburban tradition. I am now a Virginia gentleman and a historical scholar. Vive le Bourbon. Vive la Rare Book Room.' I went back upstairs and was immediately on a stage. I stood there for a whole minute after being introduced, wondering how long it would be before someone inside me opened his mouth. Once I did open my mouth I found it difficult to stop. Every poem that caught my eye seemed worth giving an airing to. I went on and on, explaining everything in clipped but incoherent phrases.

The audience was very nice about it, laughed, was quiet etc., so I leaned on the lectern and continued. I hadn't noticed that this lectern was a kind of science instructor's console on little castors and as I leant on it it spun out from under me and crashed down into the first row of seats, which were luckily empty. I brushed my hands at this and asked if anyone else felt like taking me on. This was obviously what my poetry reading was going to be 'about'. I did a little sparring while some of the students lifted my opponent back on to the podium for another round.

It was time, high time in fact, for the 'Talk on Current British Poetry' which I had rashly undertaken to give for the same fee.

'English poetry has concerned itself with the facts of feelings, American poetry with the feeling of facts,' I began tendentiously, brain reeling with the effort, exceptions leering at me from all over the place, 'English poetry has been about love and hate, death and mortality, while . . .' Here I had to stop for cigarette lighting: suddenly there seemed nothing left for American poetry to be about. I imagined Emily Dickinson looking at me quizzically. 'Do go on,' she was saying.

'American poetry is about things,' I said triumphantly, 'a love of place, of the new land . . .' My tongue kept slipping sideways off words like a tangled lariat.

I realised soon that I had embarked on a history of poetry and that I was stuck in the seventeenth century. My problem was how to bring my discourse up to date before I passed out. 'I was buried in de wars,' I wanted to explain.

Grits Ain't Groceries

'I must say you were very generous with your reading,' said the doctor's pretty wife afterwards, as we flowed out of the hall into cars and through the night to a party in a bungalow in some woods. 'I chose it from a catalogue,' a man was telling me, 'the house. It had a number. I went to Europe and when I came back there it was on stilts.' Another man called Scott Donaldson had written a book on a minor William Carlos Williams follower, Winfield Thurley Scott. 'He should have been called Winfield Thurley Winfield?' I suggested, drawing a blank.

This should have been where the girls were, but poetry never seems to be the right water for them. They are at the Godard film and the karate club. A mature-looking student introduced his wife. He talked about the New York School, so I asked him if there were any drugs to hand. First we went to someone's house where there had been a party. Some grass was dug up for the tipsy visitor and we staggered off to a truck stop for 'grits'. I can't remember what 'grits' were exactly, only their glutinous and inappropriate consistency which everyone rhapsodised over until we were asked to leave. Then,it was back to Hospitality House for the perusal of the mature-looking student's New York School poems which he happened to have about him.

Already dazed with travel, booze and dope, I read these disturbed syntheses like a credulous child. The man was a genius! Or was he a pretentious bore? His poems certainly looked original. But did this matter? I tried to remember some criteria. 'The History of Poetry' passed unwelcomely through my brain. Lines like 'staid phenomena uprooted the chinchilla patch all right' sent me groping for my iced water. I realised why certain modern poets like to live close to their mothers. I talked guardedly about texture, but my interlocutor was on top of the situation. He didn't agree with me at all. He gave me some more poems to read: the coup de grâce. I thought of running outside and burying them in the garden, but read on. Johnny, where were you when I needed you?

57

A Discreetly Period Frontage

I slept a few hours and was woken by a friendly lecturer called Tom Heacox, who insisted on writing me out the addresses of everyone he knew in America on a paper place mat while I stuffed down the huge Hospitality Breakfast (grits again). The phone rang and someone told me my next reading was impossible to arrange at such short notice. My letter hadn't arrived in time and indeed I had only just posted it. Depressed, I allowed myself to be shown the 'Wren Building', the only building in the New World designed by C. Wren. I tried to cash last night's cheque, but the bank wanted a signature verification. Tom turned up again and fixed it for me. He said I could stay the night at his cabin in the woods.

Then I was happy and wandered up the famous Duke of Gloucester Street, a reconstruction of the colonial avenue which was partly burnt down a hundred years ago. They found the original plans, demolished the newer Victorian stuff and set up this perfect-in-every-detail colonial main street, complete with milliner, wig-maker, boot-maker, even a 'music instructor'. I went into the stationer's and was amazed to see the shopkeeper in eighteenth-century clothes. I asked for one of the notebooks in the window. 'They're not for sale,' he said. 'May I see your ticket?' So this whole street was a museum! Only the camera shop, a discreetly period frontage with the single word 'FILM' in classical lettering, actually purveyed reality.

I walked a mile-long avenue to the Pump House in the pleasant late afternoon cold. Here were detached weatherboard houses with verandahs, except where the lovely 'Flemish Bond' brickwork had survived the fire. I turned back at about five when all the shopkeepers were hobbling homewards through the painterly dusk, the women bonneted and basketed, the men in frock coats and white stockings.

Poet Shaves Part of Himself

Later that night Tom's log cabin on a deserted stretch of the Chicohominy river was another reconstruction from former days: Huck Finn's raft drifting just out of sight, smoke rising in a column from somebody's camp fire. Pine needles cushioned one's footsteps right up to the front door, while pine branches made another roof over the cabin. Indoors the stove made the logs ooze perfume. My bed had a view straight over the river and I woke at dawn to see the river and sky flooded with a brilliant sunrise which filled the room with fluorescent pink light. We breakfasted on the river bank. The great dane called Oak sprang off to investigate a strange rowboat which we found to contain illicit muskrat traps.

On the way back into town we picked up a copy of the local paper. Tom found the piece about the reading and showed it to me.

'Poet shaves part of himself,' I read out.

'Shares,' said Tom. He left me at the Greyhound station and I sat there reading about myself while I waited for the bus. 'I like things to be said as they are and to mean something. I think a poem has to go somewhere,' claimed a Mr Williams.

4

GOING TO NEW ORLEANS

The Promised Land

Virginia is God's Country. It must be, it says so on the State tax allotment notices. It also has more millionaires per square mile than any other corner of the earth. I see one First Baptist Church is 'Hooked on an Ideal'. Another knows 'The Prayer of Power'. Your Southern Baptists are your genuine mad-dog red-necks, 'Prejudiced for America'. And they like to worship, if that is the word for what they do, without their slaves around to remind them of the future. When black children demonstrated by trying to attend the service in one Southern Baptist establishment, they were apprehended for disturbing the peace.

Now, this here is actually Lynchburg, Virginia. 'No getting down,' says the driver wisely. But a little boy makes it to the verge to be sick. Starcraft Apache Campers house the destitute. Alice's Beauty Mart will try to straighten their hair.

At Trailer Town a motorbike gang goes past on both sides of the bus. Pastel-coloured cars chase each other along the ridges of rocky pine hills towards Knoxville. An arrow points 'To The Barter Theater'. 'This must be Abingdon,' says my normally silent neighbour. 'The Barter was started during the Depression by a bunch of out-of-work Broadway actors. People just brought eggs, onions, chops – whatever they had. They still do it at the start of each season.' A country style 'Promised Land' comes on the radio and cheers us both. Was it fifteen minutes at Albuquerque? We've just been allowed ten minutes in Bristol. Grey-haired men sniff the pornography in the deserted station.

One wears a crucifix outside his red shirt, while reading an ad for hairy legs. Across the street is a red-painted 'Magic-Touch' massage parlour, with 'all-girl staff' – tiny and shut.

'The YMCA is for you and me.' No, it's not. Half-bricks, broken bottles, old silencers, aerosols litter the yard, but 'Open Your Eyes to Another World', says the advert, as Brenda Lee sings 'Something's Wrong with Me'. I suppose someone up there will plough over all this mineral excess bedaubing America in the end, but in the meantime . . . 'Get Your Kicks in the Hillbilly World', 'Buy some – Grade A Pasteurised Homogenised Vitamin D White Pet Milk', 'Visit the Smoky Pig Disco', 'The Convenience Market', 'Pepsi Welcomes You to Washington County'. Spaciously laid out weatherboard bungalows. Mowing machines big as dodgems. Foot-long hot-dogs for $1. 'Take a Camera and See Rock City', 'Millions have seen Rock City – have you?' How can I with no camera? 'Zirkle Rainwater Auctioneers: A Sale of Night Crawlers.' A house turning slowly on top of a pole is an ad for Rolling Acres Inc. 'Put your hand on your radio,' says the disc-jockey, 'feel the warmth of my sincerity.'

Everyone gets down, and I look on the postcard to find out where we are. So, this is Knoxville. Time to ring Dick Tarrant in Nashville. You come half way across the world, bump into a stranger in a strange town, who gives you another stranger's name like a kind of password. You travel another thousand miles, ring him out of the blue and as if by some miracle of human faith this second stranger agrees to meet you off the bus in a white Barracuda.

Roads clear and easy now. There goes Chattanooga. Cream and brown sunset like the South Downs. Untamed wooded ways. It's better than television. Knees up, eyes wide, I glide across America in a Silver Eagle Stratocruiser. What must it have been like for the first settlers to come upon this temperate paradise at last – more and endlessly more of it like a sign from God that all was well? In Australia hundreds of men lost their lives searching for a New Virginia over the next dreadful horizon. But there was no Virginia, only Alice Springs. And there was no revolution – only Test Matches. The Americans haven't done badly turning their Promised Land into a Wilderness, however. Under a blinking star a Holiday Inn 'Welcomes Boss and Secretary'. Now here is Dickie Tarrant to get me . . .

He took me to Thursdays. It was Saturday night – old-time gaudy with enormous men and women shouting and drinking out of mugs with lids like Germans. The red-tinted flesh of the girls was absolutely bursting out of sixties minis and twinnies like double hamburgers tartare. Now here was Francie in hot-pants and this was Sharon. Sharon likes European men! OK, fine. Hello Sharon. Who is this though? This? Ah, this is Jackie. Jackie works here. Two beers, Jackie, and make it today. So you like Thursdays, William? Yes. We drank more beer and went out to find somewhere to eat. Sharon was with us, and Lucy in her Chevrolet. Her small face was expressionless, but she had the words 'Led Zeppelin' strung like a Welcome sign between two death-defying tits. I tried to decipher this palimpsest. I knew the meaning of what was hidden. It was the surface message that was difficult. Led Zeppelin, let me see – heavy (straight), sixties (sex), English (me!). I moved along the seat.

'Do you like Blue Grass music?' asked Lucy.

'Yes.' We had arrived at the Blue Grass Inn. Inside a large bare-boarded shed, fold-away chairs and tables were scattered away from a rough stage where some people were playing very fast on fiddles. Beers arrived. 'They are all a family,' said Lucy. 'Hubert Travis and the Season Travellers. That's the daughter on bass. The mother sings, and the boy plays the banjo. They're the best! They'll play their hit, "Rocky Top", soon!' The music reminded me of hearty Caledonian Society dances at school. I had a short conversation about folk music with Lucy, after which she said she preferred Neil Diamond. I remembered the T-shirt – I hadn't read the small print: 'The opinionated need not apply.' Then Lucy went to talk to the band and I found myself with Sharon.

Just for a Coffee

'Hello, did you like the group?'

'Very much.'

'I prefer country. This your first time in the States?' Sharon was ample, Mediterranean, Sal Mineo with hips.

'Do you live at home?'

'Yes. But my mother doesn't care what I do and Dad's

always asleep. He's not well. They were in a crash last year –
both drunk. I found them lying beside the road. Lucy bought
the car afterwards, but we both use it.'

We ordered some salads and fried chicken. Dick and Lucy
were talking to the band in the dressing-room.

'How long you staying in Nashville?'

'Till tomorrow, I think.'

'We can go to my place if you like. Just for a coffee, you
know . . .'

'Yes, I know.'

'Mum works in the Bowling. I have to feed the dogs.'

She went over to get Lucy's car keys. I moved my case out of
Dick's car and we drove out of the town with the roof down.
Soon we were at a high-rise apartment block. In the lift Sharon
told me to take my shoes off. Coming out of the lift on the
eighteenth floor, there was a magnificent view over the lights of
Nashville. I felt exhilarated and started kissing Sharon. We
tiptoed down the hall and into the apartment. It was very small
and shabby. The living-room door was open and her father was
asleep on a divan. Sharon started pouring some drinks and he
sat bolt upright and peered around him. When he saw us he put
his finger to his lips. 'Your mother's in there with your Granny.
They came home early. She's locked the door.'

'Have you fed the dogs?'

'No.' She showed me where her bedroom was and said she'd
be with me in a minute. A bed filled the tiny room. Stars and
street lights filled the window. The walls were covered with
black polythene. There were piles of comics jammed down
between the bed and the walls. I could hear a woman snoring
slightly through paper thin walls. I stood there, sure that I
was about to have this madonna-like girl. I started to get
undressed.

'Are you in the toilet?' came Sharon's whisper from outside
the door.

'No, I'm here,' I said, opening the door. It was Sharon's
mother in her nightgown, her hair sticking out in papers. She
saw me standing there in my underpants and she screamed.
She closed the door quickly and all hell broke loose. The dog
started barking and woke Granny who started cursing Sharon's
father. The mother was screaming abuse at Sharon. 'You little
whore. Get that man out of here.' Sharon came back into the

63

room to defend me. Everyone was talking to each other as if the thin walls didn't exist.

'OK, Mother, just give us five minutes.'

'No. I won't give you five minutes, you dirty little slut. How dare you!'

'She's not usually like this,' said Sharon. 'She's taking pills.'

'I'd better creep out.'

'No, I'll come with you.'

'Is he going now or not?'

'Tell him I'd like a word with him before he goes,' came Granny's croak from next door. She seemed to think Sharon's father was being kicked out.

'Let him stay till I get my clothes on. He owes me ten bucks.'

This enraged Sharon's father, who had been pretending to be asleep. He got up and started banging on her door and jangling some change. Now it was Granny who was in trouble. I said I'd better leave, but Sharon, who liked European men, insisted on coming with me.

'We'll go round to Louie's,' she said.

I thought this might be a bar, but it turned out to be a friend, who came to the door with a towel round his waist. He nodded and nodded to everything Sharon said, then showed us into the spare room.

'I'll just have a word with Louie,' said Sharon. 'He's depressed about his exams.' She went out and I saw I was in some kind of recording studio. Guitars lay everywhere. A vibraphone was arranged across the small bed. I got undressed. Half an hour later Sharon hadn't returned. I opened the door and heard sounds of creaking bed-springs coming from Louie's bedroom. I shifted the vibraphone from the bed and went to sleep.

Nashville-itis

Next morning Dick dropped me on the slip-road to the Memphis freeway and I tried to get a lift.

'What you doing here boy? Don't you know there's no bumming on the freeway?'

I showed the police my passport and they ran me back to the Greyhound. Two hours to wait for the next bus to Memphis and only one shop open on Sundays. I went in and bought postcards of Teddy and Doyle Wilburn, chubby country singers in red silk tuxedos and dickies.

'It's a nice picture of the boys,' said the woman.

'Are they local boys?' I asked, as she overcharged me on a Rancho-style Tru-Western dickie I was buying as well.

'Oh no, they're international. Doyle's always in and out of here.'

'Which is Doyle now?'

'This one.'

'I thought that was Teddy,' I said, pointing to the name on his guitar.

'You Canadian or something?'

I'm sitting in the Greyhound station again, writing the post-cards. Over the road is the Canary Bar where the prostitutes come and go, their vicious dark pimps lurking outside to slap their bottoms.

'I wish I had a figure like that,' says a fat girl sitting next to me, as a negress in yellow satin shorts takes the arm of a white businessman. 'My body aches all over, you know. I can't stop it aching. Where you heading?'

'Memphis.' She rubs her immense bottom at the thought of my journey.

'Whad'ya wanna come to a dump like Nashville for?'

'Well, you hear about Nashville, I've always wanted to come here.'

'O yeah, Paul McCartney came here didn't he? My father was a guitarist. He died of strangulation. Yeah, asphyxiation, that's it. They suspected my mother. I had to say she was with me. He was sick at the time. Then my mother dies of multiple sclerosis. I don't know what I'm dying of. Nashville-itis! No. I'm not going anywhere. Can't afford to. I just come down here to get away. I'd like to go to Oklahoma City. But I'm aching all over . . .' She has to get a meal. I see her tucking into the rich food. Later she is sitting on a wall talking to a black pimp, an envious, longing-to-be-sold look in her eye as she watches the tarts working.

'ALL ABOARD FOR MEMPHIS. NO DRINKING PLEASE. SMOKERS OCCUPY THE REAR SEATS THANK YOU.'

Memphis, Tennessee

The Tennessee Hotel, Memphis, has a prayer ten feet high over the doorway: 'Whosoever therefore shall confess me before men him will I confess before my father which is in heaven.' A card near the phone says 'Relax at the Derby Club. Enjoy the Ultimate in Sensitivity Sessions at the Lowest Prices. Coconut Milk Whirlpool. Pulsating Jet Shower. Knicks and Ranger Games on Closed Circuit. Credit Cards.'

I sit in my room listening to the local radio. The mayor of Memphis has made a diabolical pop record promoting tourism in the area. Beginning with the words 'Long distance operator, this *is* Memphis, Tennessee', it is conceived as a response to Chuck Berry's classic. Now the singing mayor comes on to chat about his recording debut. No, he doesn't consider he is making a fool of himself and his town. I listen amazed and can't help imagining the dismay of Berry's anxious caller trying to get in touch with his young daughter and finding himself instead the recipient of this old geezer's paltry doggerel extolling the touristic facilities of the place.

But then I imagine Philistines all over the world must turn and face Memphis when they pray. In the square named after her second most famous son, W.C. Handy, there is a statue of the black composer. Near it a rough-hewn concrete gents has been thrown down. 'W.C. Handy – geddit?' nudged my awful companion.

The air-conditioned White Rose Café for breakfast. It was full of puffy males crammed into jackets and garotted with their own ties. I heard the words 'no shirt . . . shirt . . . no shirt . . .' coming from several throats at the sight of my jacket and T-shirt as I threaded through the tables. Good, a little paranoia with the coffee should set me up. I stared back as others at the tables turned round to give me the gimlet. I found out later that these venerable souls were members of the Mid-South Cotton Growers Association and that they had come across from the Chamber of Commerce opposite the café. There was talk of cotton and the mayor. Cigarettes, those companions of the odd-man-out, were unlikely to disappear, I reflected, so long as such men went on burying their teeth in ham that way. My order took hours. As I smoked my way into a residency, I began to realise that the place was segregated by sex, not just colour.

Females were being shown to a small area behind a screen. I wondered where blacks would be shown. I had stumbled on some fabulous outpost of the good old days. I could see it preserved for posterity in a wax-works, the wax-like flesh of its clientele frozen in grimaces of distrust, the harpy-featured waitress bearing them cups of blood.

The Land of Sleep

'You a keroot?' said the man with a clip board at the bus station. I had to get him to say it three times before I realised what he was saying. Recruits! Here I was drifting down America and there were these poor bastards being rounded up for the army. I felt my identity start to slide again. You're looking out of a window and you see a man going past looking at the street numbers. You watch him, and as he looks up at you for a second you see yourself through his eyes, a face in a window, part of the background. For three-quarters of the time that is the experience of travelling.

The doors close with a wheezing clunk. In the dim light of the bus garage the dark forms of mothers with children loom down the aisle, looking for a place. The big bus moves majestically into sunlight. Giant Foods of America has a statue of a giant darkie carrying the packages. Beside the 'Jump 'n Grab Grocer's' a little shack houses Madame Rose, palmist. Rich farm land starts. Muddy plough tracks make for the horizon in the smokey stillness. Three blue planes wait outside Bob Carr's Aircraft Sales. Welcome to Clarksdale. Now Parking for over 22,000 cars! The town consists of earth, adverts, shacks, cars, a Holiday Inn saying 'We salute Pride of Cotton Week', a church: 'The Rev. Daniel Pale, Pastor. A Black Independent Church' and a McDonald's, 'Over 16 Billion Served'. Scrapped automobiles mount one another in desperate copulation at Sam's Success Story. The ubiquitous Mr Block, Income Tax Specialist, is much in evidence. But the Hep Ur Sef drive-in mart is defunct. At the bus stop on the outskirts a motley crew of blacks wait with demented expressions and their hats on crooked. The women's hair has been straightened then curled again. They make to get on the bus, they change their minds.

Sky low over the poor jungle town of Greenwood, ads towering over the bungalows, everything run-down but the roads.

The Part-time Virgin is on at the Sportatorium drive-in. Barefoot boys hang round the Day and Night Auto Parts. 'This district has gone 1848 days with no disabling accident.' Great heavy drifts of old man's beard clog the trees. But they're bound to call it something else in America.

Now its Tchula (read off the Town Hall). The little shacks are all below and subservient to the highway, except the Unitarian Chapel: 'Grow in Grace, Not Groan in Disgrace'. Trees grow in water. A herd of black cattle on green. A line of six school buses moves over for us. Yazoo next, with Sonny's Salvage Store the hub, and Sister Martin's House of Prayer over by the horse-mount. These depressed little townships of Mississippi seem cut off from America and each other. Do the woods line the road, or was the road hacked through them? Ugly evidence of an oilfield under construction. On to Bolin where a tri-county baseball match is underway: red caps, blue and white sports suits in a sweltering field, ads for Mississippi's Petrified Forest. Johnny Green is on his way from New Orleans: his band and girls. 'Ladies Free Now' at Epp's Cabaret. The Williams Lounge is 'The Land of Fun'. A black workers' housing estate sinks into mud near the orange girders of a new bridge at Scott's Trading Post. But Jackson is a white town with planted trees, colonial porches, a Hotel King Edward and the car for cathedral. I try to phone my friend in New Orleans but someone in the booth is talking to Mother: 'I'm just so excited to walk down State Street again. I'm just going to walk up and down till I believe I'm home' (Americans have a lot of trouble believing things that happen to them) and I nearly miss the bus. We pull out past the littered site of a future Planetarium with 'Let's Get into Cotton this Year'. The Suburban Lounge advertises its Family Plan, while Days Inn has The Tasty Word. The Controlled Air Comfort Co. is in business, as is The Pollution Control Project. A hoarding at the edge of Jackson proclaims 'The Land of Sleep'. A hard, dark forest sets in. The spaces between the trees have the look of having been cleared only temporarily by man.

At Crystal a plaque explains how the town moved three miles west to the new railroad in 1858. A handbell waits outside a lonely church. At the unattended gas station a note advises 'look for a twist or bend in the hose if gas will not pump'. Some black boys dig for worms.

Night falling and the driver is making loud observations on cat-fishing to nobody in particular. He's getting nearer home. Now he remembers how his wife beats him. She broke his nose three times in a month. He shows his profile to his sleeping passengers.

At the centre of Hazlehurst, 'The Fruit Stand' (four poles and some corrugated iron)has got both Coke *and* Pepsi to do a sign for it. Magnolia trees in a leafy suburb, and just behind it, the car-dump in a ravine, lianas tangling them like the temples of Angkor Wat. At Brockhaven the First Church of God confronts The American Oil Company. Fir trees now, long sun, better road, 'Your Highway Taxes have been used as follows . . .' But the lack of crossing roads suggests vast cotton estates hidden from view. Summit, Missouri, is the prettiest town so far: graceful dwellings among trees, arcade shopping, but deserted-looking like a lot of these oases. Can it still be the evening meal?

Now we have stopped and the driver has slung the name of the place over his shoulder as usual and as usual I can't understand it. Getting out, I asked him to repeat it. 'I jes tol yer.' 'I beg your pardon?'

Tornado Watch

On my arrival in New Orleans I rang up one Jerome Gysin. He was in Baton Rouge studying poultry, but his wife said I was to stop over all the same and had I eaten yet? I got in a taxi and was soon face to face with Su-Su Gysin, a pale, fat young woman with a hard face and slow, kind movements. She made a fry-up and watched me eating it with birdlike envy. She talked a lot about the heat and the weakness of the current driving the many fans in our faces. She was on a diet of figs and liver and it made her sweat, which I could see, and the pills made her toilet conscious, she told me.

She went off to have a cold shower and came back wearing a pink shortie nightie and carrying a tray of cold tea and pills. There was something in her hair for dandruff.

'I'm going to try to go to bed,' she announced. 'You know it takes me all day to get back to bed again in the night. The air's like treacle. I'm starving . . .'

A girl came on the box and sang a satirical song called 'Glory

69

Glory Psychotherapy As the Id Goes Marching On'. Su-Su and I went upstairs.

'There's a Tornado Watch tonight,' she said hopefully. 'But that isn't the same thing as a Tornado Warning.'

I was to keep my door open so she could breathe, she said.

'Have a Shitty Day'

Bus down Canal Street to Rampart. I feel my way into the French Quarter and begin a daylong walk up Royal, down Bourbon, along Toulouse, searching, searching for the key to my late arrival in this mythical city, 'preserved', yet not preserved against the ravages of time and the devil.

The streets are lined with strip-joints and rainbow rooms, with togged-up Dixie bands playing the Saints all day to busloads from Miami and Japan. Clarence 'Frogman' Henry is still singing and Ernie K. Doe is due. But Louis Armstrong and Fats Domino came from another place. The lovely wrought-iron balconies have been colonised with neon.

'Everything in this establishment is guaranteed non-antique,' says a sign in a shop window. 'Everything here is glorified junk. What you buy is glorified, what you leave is junk.' I visit a Voodoo museum and see a sleeping rattlesnake. The town isn't happening to me. It's after my money but has nothing I want. T-shirts on droopy US bosoms advise me to 'HAVE A SHITTY DAY'. 'America was here', it says on a toilet wall somewhere.

Walking to the Café du Monde in a new arcade by the river, I see a possible lonely co-star leaving, so I don't go in. She has false eyelashes, vacant movements like me and long white legs in shorts. I follow her back towards the centre. She flutters this way and that like a tempting fly pulled back and forth across a pool by a fisherman. Men nose towards her absent-mindedly and are left behind. She sees nothing. But she trails a certain brightness. She glances at the portrait painter, crosses the park where the hippies say 'Hey, man' to their headbands, re-enters the street and seems to wake up among the crowds. The street is a mirror of windows and eyes for her. She knows I am there and she tilts me this way and that, catching a glimpse of herself as she turns down Bourbon Street again. If I could touch her I could touch the town. To get the person in the street to recognise you opens up the fourth dimension of a place. I cross the street a few times in a fever of displacement activity, then block her way as she comes out of a tourist shop. Not a trace of surprise passes across her face. Her world is already alive with such encounters. She opens her mouth and I see the word 'Hi' on her heart-shaped lips. We do a little bird-dance on the steps. I try to make it look as if I am with her as she moves around me to get away. But she is not confused. Would she like a drink? No, no! Go to the back of the class! A coffee? She's just eaten. What terrible sense that makes. We walk and I mutter in my foreign tongue. No good reeling in if the fish won't bite. She goes into a gallery. If I don't follow maybe she will regret it. I walk on and a minute later she comes out. Of course, nothing for her in there. I wander after her, exhausted with tension, my heart going like a hammer from not knowing what my body is going to do next. Now she enters the Wildlife Museum. I should follow her, but I wait outside on the wall. When she comes out I ask where she is going. That's a wet one, but I am sulking now. I see the word 'home' coming from her mouth without a sound to encourage me. We have ruined each other's mornings.

I walk for a while without taking anything in, then unexpectedly start to feel better for having dared to enter the void for once, if only to check that it was empty. Adrenalin has caused an hour to fly past. It's not the outcome but the asking that clears the air.

To Julie Jones

At the post office there was no word from Julie Jones. I'd been given her address in Canada and had written asking her to leave a note for me. I looked her up in the book and found I'd got the wrong address. After a whole morning walking past her house on Rue Royal I wandered up some stairs and through the open door of her apartment, where she was walking towards me, saying my name and asking if I'd like a Dixie beer. She'd got my letter that very day and had been half expecting me. I had left the street and found the town. Here were three connecting rooms like a Vermeer. ('It's called a walk-up shotgun! You can shoot straight through it,' said Julie.) A wrought-iron balcony framed a magnolia in the front of the Wildlife Museum opposite, where an hour earlier I had sat waiting for a stranger to cut me dead.

Julie's smile was a strange, down-dragging Bogart movement of the mouth which challenged you to make something of it, then changed before your eyes into hospitality. I was dying for a smoke so she found some stale Kools for me and a damp box of Biba matches. Then we sat talking about London and I realised I had heard of her there. When I was working on the *London Magazine* a story came in by Alexander Theroux, dedicated to one Julie Jones. I wouldn't have noticed this, but when Theroux came in with the corrected proof we found he had dedicated the story to a different girl. Three days later he re-appeared full of contrition and wanted the dedication changed back again. 'Julie Jones,' he said, 'I love that girl.' Julie was most interested in all this and kept asking who the other girl was, but I couldn't remember. She told me his last book had been dedicated to the Holy Ghost, a more abiding muse.

Are we getting on? I never know. She tells me she was depressed in London. After three years a friend told her to pack up and go home and I wondered if I was an unwelcome reminder of that time. By the way, never ask academics if they write: a long silence, downhill. Julie is chief English Lecturer at New Orleans University. She will publish things on Joyce and Yeats, but only to keep her job and in academic journals. It seems they sack everyone after five years to avoid giving them tenure (unless they become famous). I couldn't imagine this happening to lovely shining intelligent fading Julie, but she was looking sulky at her prospects now. When the plot gets too complicated, said Raymond Chandler, have a man come through the door with a gun. But it wasn't a man with a gun, it was Julie's aunt with a poodle that had to be walked. I volunteered. While I'm out it comes on to rain and I shelter in a bakery, feeling as if I've lived here for years with my poodle that everyone seems to know. It has been one of those days where everything seems to have been made up five minutes before. And the people have a strong vitality, stronger than my own. When I get back to the flat Julie's aunt is taking instant photos. There's one of me holding the dog and looking with dog-like eyes at Julie: the wrong expression.

Banana Bread

Su-Su, my hostess, was baking banana bread. She was taking food and clothes to some poor relations across the river and asked me if I wanted to go with her. The relatives didn't ask us into their tiny neo-colonial cottage, but came out on to the stoop as for a census count, a big family of poor whites, holding babies and drying their hands on aprons. One curtseyed. We handed over the things and retreated sideways to the air-conditioned car, Su-Su obviously gratified by the effect.

On the way back we passed some blacks fooling around with an Alsatian. One of them had a piece of board upraised. The puppy was bounding about. This enraged Su-Su. She circled back and wound down the window.

'What you think you doin' beatin' on that dawg?' she shrieked. I was wondering whether to lock all the doors or make a run for it.

'We're not beatin' on the dawg, ma'am.'

'Don't give me none of that back-talking. What you doin' with that hunk a wood?'

'We're jes training him ma'am. Training him fer the police.'

'Fer the police is it? We'll see about that. Just you come over hyar.' Just then a police car drew up.

'Wind down your window, Hugo.'

'Having some trouble, ma'am?'

'Officer, my name is Gysin. You remember me? Officer Franks and myself . . . Now these boys were beating on this dawg. If there's one thing I can't abide . . .' The officer looks dubious, though he does what he's told and pulls over to grill the blacks, who approach the police car to explain, hanging their heads, the dog bounding after them. I can't believe this scene. Was it all for me? Or was this standard treatment. Su-Su turns to me for my reactions.

'Anyway, I never heard of training a dawg that way before.' Pause. 'You known my daddy says I ain't afraid of the devil.'

'You're incredible.'

'I'm a honky bitch. I know that. I ain't about to take no lip from no sambo. I had a crossed line the other day. A picka-ninny. He called me a bitch, so I told him I was a honky bitch. That's what they call us, you know.'

73

Su-Su drops me near Bourbon Street and I wander into the noise and light, relieved to get away.

The Mating Season

The first thing I see is the Sho-Bar, a seedy night-spot with a fifties rock show advertised outside. It was closed, but the door was open and I could see girls in bobby-sox and pony-tails rehearsing 'Rockin' Robin': a place to come back to. I locate The Dungeon and Crazy Shirley's, both recommended but still closed, then find a place to eat oysters off the messy counter at Felix's, where the man alongside me says they ain't salty enough. Fat, tasteless, exploding grey matter, eaten with huge amounts of tomato sauce, tabasco, horse radish and saltine biscuits to lay them on. $1.50 for six.

'They're like that 'cos it's the mating season,' says the man.

'Thanks.' He stuffs them away.

'Make good stewing oysters though.'

The Storyville Jazz band brays for nobody at Crazy Shirley's – a bucket for tips – doors flung open on the busy street, as they are to endless burlesque nude bars with buskers holding aside the curtain for you to see sundry spotlit tits and bums clenched in time to the Bee Gees. Straight nudes . . . the bottomless bar . . . men and women on show . . . also all-boy cabaret. One has big tits. Probably a woman. One rabid transvestite devil stands in the street near by insulting everyone who passes. 'You cat-sucker,' he says to someone who tells him his prick is hanging out (which it is). The legs of a girl on a swing poke again and again out of a first-floor window – a curiosity which achieved some acclaim in this jaded city. Another place has the same idea, but false legs pushing through felt. You can just see that there is no body. Steve Valenti's Paddock Lounge has 'Steve Valenti'. The Office is crowded full. Le Downtowner Motor Lodge is built in agonising good taste – neo-French Quarter. Looking up, I'm surprised to see weekending couples looking down on the throbbing night from the calm and intimacy of their Hilton balconies, drinks in hand as they are in the hands of many people walking down here in Bourbon Street. I see they are shifting the barricades of seats from across Rue Royal, the shopping, daytime place, to Bourbon, the nightly promenade. Soon it fills to the brim with tourists, sauntering with Planters in their hands, their necks on swivels. I tried to roll a joint at Crazy Shirley's but none of these places has toilets with doors. Out in the street I get so far with it but can't do the last bit and have to give up. Having checked out all the music including the fearful Top Hat Banjo Band at Your Father's Moustache – motorway amusements – I decide on the rock 'n roll show at the Sho-Bar.

Wet Dollars

Of course, it was empty. But I immediately liked the place – the ghost of Vaudeville instead of Burlesque as elsewhere. They got a new dance and it goes like this . . . At the Hop, Great Balls of Fire, 'This is Rick Fain and the Fascinations. Friends of his anyway. Turkey on saxophone. Take a bow sir.' Nobody applauds. There are just three sailors and a drunk and me. 'Love Potion No. 9', 'Hound Dog', 'Johnny B. Goode'. I was laughing at the girls fighting over Turkey during his solo in 'In the Still of the Night' when two black girls came in. I laughed harder and they sat down in the next booth to me. When they looked over I said how much I liked the group. They agreed. Then one of them asked would I like to date. 'Yes,' I said, thinking my enthusiasm must be catching.

'How would you like to date two girls?'

'Of course!' What fun, two black girls to go around with. What would they like to drink, asked the black waitress who had a packet of More on her tips tray. 'You, honey,' said one of them to her. But they had Southern Comforts on me. I had all my dollars and maps and cigarette papers spread tipsily across the table and when my beer came I managed to spill it over their legs trying to pay. When they came back from the john I asked them where they lived. Chicago. And what did they do here? 'We date.'

'What's that?' I asked, thinking of some kind of market research or promotion.

'Partying, you know. We party. Together or alone.' I still hadn't twigged.

'Isn't it difficult?' I asked, remembering friends who used to rely on deb dinner parties for their tri-weekly blow-outs.

'Not here in New Orleans.'

'You like it here?'

'Wouldn't stay here unless I liked it, would we? Anywhere's OK for us. You wanna date or what?'

'How much?', I asked, tumbling at last to the changed tone of her voice.

'$40 – $20 for her and $20 for me, OK?'

I starting counting the wet dollars on the table top. There were fifteen. They repaired once more to the toilet to confer.

'You got a place?' enquired the negotiator.

'No.'

'OK. It's been nice knowing ya. Bye.'

I got another beer and was enjoying myself even more, having escaped the inevitable let-down by a probable mere $5's breadth – and no strength of my own. I didn't even notice that the show was repeating itself. It was high evening now and in between numbers the blonde girl in the line-up kept running past me into the street where she seemed to be handing out cards to the passers-by. A huddle of Japanese businessmen came in and a few shouting English tourists. The blonde and the lead singer, a brunette, went behind me during one of the intervals and I called out 'You're great!' Two minutes later the brunette came over. 'Can I sit down?' Her name was Mona, the others were Jessie-Bell and Rose-Allison. I said I loved the show and hated all the other joints in New Orleans. Why was the place empty? Well, this was 'B' company, she explained, spawned by one Lance Lynch, now in LA with the original Fascinations. Plus the tourists preferred the funky junk just now. Up came the blonde one, Rose.

'We'd been wondering where all our groupies were,' she said.

'Well, we're here,' I said. I had stumbled on a role at last: Fan! I was a member of the tribe, however broadly defined. No longer taboo. Other ways of gaining membership might be 'Didn't I see you last week at . . . ?', 'Haven't we met somewhere before . . . ?' or, as in this case, a complex exchange of musical references and preferences. But how was I doing? It didn't seem to matter too much. The thrill they got from performing was carrying us along with it like a brush fire. We had a three-way talk for a while, then Mona slunk off. Rose told me they had all seen me enjoying myself and had been singing for me. But what was I doing talking to those hookers? I said I didn't realise they were hookers. 'Fucking cheek,' said Rose, 'taking our audience!' Then: 'I laughed so much when you poured your drink over them . . . where you staying?'

She kept dashing off to sing then coming back for a cigarette. I was just about to suggest going to The Dungeon after the show when she said she'd meet me there the following night.

The Adaptor

Bedtime at Su-Su's. I switch the tv off and Su-Su fetches the tray of cold limeade and crackers. At the top of the stairs we fork right and left. I am to leave my door open for the draught, but the cat rushes straight in and starts searching in my suit-case for the grass that is hidden there. I lie on the 'nun's bed'. A red dog stares at me from on top of the wardrobe, beside a bleak Mardi Gras bowler. Under the bed a dismantled chandelier jingles occasionally. Su-Su calls.

'You busy Hugo? You mind putting this fan on top of the closet for me? I've gotten this other one here, but the flex is too short. Maybe if I had the adaptor in your room I could fix this one nearer the bed.' I fetch the adaptor. 'Gee I'm stiff from driving. You wanna drink? We could put some rum in this.' She pours me a drink and starts redeploying the powerful gales around the room. The atmosphere is suddenly like black-socked pornography: talk is formal but Su-Su has on a lacy day-coat over a nightie and she swirls about with her eyelashes still on.

'Look', she announces sensibly, 'I know I'm not going to sleep with this back.' She has plugged a home-massage device into the adaptor near the bed. 'Would you mind running this over my shoulders a few times, Hugo? I feel like I'm all twisted up back here. Maybe a pinched nerve . . .'

I take the juddering attachment into my hands as if I am receiving stolen goods. Su-Su takes off her day-coat and lies face down on the high bed. I sit wielding the unfamilar object and she groans with satisfaction. 'Thank God for that. That's just great. Keep on there. Here . . .' She takes down the shoul-der strap, 'Run it down my back.' She moans to herself and I realise that quite soon now I shall have to make a decision. I look at her legs spread slightly apart, one bent at the knee. Who is having this idea? OK then, let's see what happens. With my free hand I pull her nightdress up to her waist. That's it. She doesn't do anything. How did she know I was a push-over?

The Dungeon

Next evening I went with Julie via the Napoleon House where John Crowe Ransom's grandson works as a waiter, to Johnny Matassas, to hear James Carroll Booker III play the piano. We also pass the house of one of New Orleans's famous eccentrics, The Virgin Mary, who used to carry a small cross around with her and pull a little truck. When she died nobody knew who her house belonged to, so the Church claimed it. Julie told me about another French Quarter character called Levy Lady who dressed in rags and drank heavily, until one day she appeared sober in a smart red costume.

Johnny Matassas, the first real music spot I had seen in the town, was empty of course, but Booker's piano playing, blues filtered through a classical style, was so enjoyable we sat for hours drinking and talking in elegiac terms about London. After his set, Booker, wearing a black suit and a black eye patch with a diamanté star, stood up and said to the eight people present: 'If anyone like to lay a drink on me that'd be very welcome.' I remember his best tune was one called 'Slow but Sure'.

It was time for Julie to go home. I had two hours to kill before meeting Rose at The Dungeon. Feeling tired with the recent drinks wearing off I thought to get some food inside me at that Café du Monde, but there were only doughnuts. At the back was the Mississippi and the sunset. An attractive notice board announced a 'Moon Walk' along the riverbank: 'See the Sunset from HERE!' Hey! That's a neat idea, fellas. We can look at the river to our right, see the historic town of Noo Orlins on our left.

I joined five Japanese men eating hamburgers in the Busy Bee Grill and enjoyed their discreet company for a couple of cigarettes. They worked for 'Mandarin orange canning factory, Osaka' they told me, eyelids twitching, and their product had 'new improved flavour'.

'Try it, you'll like,' they assured me, handing over a large tin of the insipid fruit. Just what I needed for The Dungeon.

'You bring from Japan?'

'No, no. Of course!'

One of them had on an Old Etonian tie. Later I saw them all leaning forward from the waist to look into Eskimo Nell's Bottomless Igloo.

By the time I reached The Dungeon Rose was already there talking slightly drunkenly to Pres Bird, a swinging guy who gave me a counter for as many free drinks as I could hold, as I was a friend of a friend of his.

'Pres loves anything to do with music,' said Rose as progressive guitar solos blistered the woodwork.

'You're nervous,' she said, her arm round Pres's neck. 'Don't be nervous in Noo Orlins. You have to hang loose. Jus rock out like Pres 'n me.'

Now Pres took us upstairs to see his pride and joy, the disco. He did his show for us standing behind the bar. A mask oozed up and down. A worm of cups with a furry head slowly revolved. Pres's own face lit up from above and below alternately as he slowed down, speeded up, then suddenly increased the volume to an incredible pitch, quickly changing back and forth from various British solo artists, suddenly cutting it all off for a train screeching from speaker to speaker, all the time searching my tense face for a plausible reaction. I gave myself the count of three, then roared with laughter, seemingly to myself, finally bellowing a gigantic 'great' over the thunder. Pres was delighted I was delighted and Rose was delighted Pres was delighted we were all delighted. So I had three more Wild Turkey Bourbons, having seen a wild turkey in the Louisiana Wildlife Museum inside the Law Courts earlier that day. Rose too was throwing them back. I kept getting the splendid bulges of her body in the chest and groin as we shrieked at one another over the obliterating sound levels. Talk tends to be about groups when the music is that noticeable: it's the only trustworthy shorthand for togetherness. My head must be stuffed with the names of more cracked singers and defunct rock 'n roll bands than the BBC archives. I sometimes feel like chucking it all out and starting again on botany or something.

'Have you seen the wood anemones?'

'I'm not sure. Who do they sound like?'

Necking and kissing repeatedly, I was given a whole range of no's to choose from by Rose. (1) She had a virtuous reputation, i.e. she didn't just fall into bed. And I believed her. (2) She shared rooms with the two other girls. And I believed that too. (3) It was even the wrong time of the month, so if I wasn't put off after that I must be all right.

As it turned out the only reason she had for hesitating was

the appalling stink and squalor of her pad. But I wasn't to know that then.

Once outside The Dungeon, I signalled a cab for her. But she didn't want it now and we went on smooching down the street like everyone else in sight – necking in doorways at 4 a.m. in the still busy Bourbon Street, until it slowly became clear that we could go to her place now. We got in a cab and she started telling me how incredibly squalid her place was. I said I hoped it was really really squalid, but she wasn't joking. An apartment kidded out of a jerrybuilt outhouse off a back yard somewhere, it had a padlock, a smashed door, a broken shower room with black tiles and no ceiling, packing cases, beds blocking the door to a tiny, fake room smelling horrible. The far end of the room had false panelling halfway up the wall and a fake fireplace leaning dangerously forward into the room. Against the wall, there was a treacherous-looking sofa. The thick brown carpet was full of detritus. An air-conditioner instead of a window. Over the bed the ceiling was missing again. While Rose was in the shower I put my face to the bed and was relieved to find it smelt only of bed. Rose also, when she came out of the bathroom, smelt of nothing but teenage lust. I buried my face in her white flesh and tried with complete success to blot out everything else for a minute or two before Mona arrived with Turkey and they started bulging around together on the sofa.

Pills for Ills

I woke up feeling distinctly ill. My throat was sore and my bones ached. I struggled back home and there was Su-Su in the process of phoning the police about my 'disappearance'. The last time someone stayed with her she had to go and get them out of gaol, she said.

I went into the bathroom and started going through her medicine cupboard for possible antibiotics. I must have been stupid with fever. There were numerous double-coloured pills and I took one of each. An hour later I had to get up and pee a very little bright green liquid, and again every half hour for the rest of the day. In my fever I had swallowed Su-Su's anaemia and slimming pills. One of them, called Apotil, was something to make fatties thin by peeing too much. I was up and down all night, thirsty with fever, unable to hold it, unable to stay warm and sweat it out in bed, continually banging the door to keep out the howling air-conditioners and hearing murmurings of protest coming from Su-Su's bedchamber, while the cats kept up their zealous search for drugs among the possessions spilling out of my suitcase.

It was during this interlude that I became aware of the disturbing, high-pitched voice of the black Reverend 'Rosyfelt' Franklin pumping some old momma on the radio about the benefits she had had from his True Blue Prosperity Package. I managed to put the machine on 'record'. The words still make me feel slightly feverish:

– God bless you God bless you. Then what you were saying is your son was on this er dope thing is that right?

– That stuff they call it speed.

– He was on speed and now things have seemed to change greatly for the better is that right?

– Right, the whole thing has changed.

– And you are well pleased and satisfied?

– Pleased and satisfied since I been corresponding with you everything has worked out just like you told me it would do.

– God bless you God bless you. Now as far as the dope, about how much was he do you think spending a day for this dope?

– Over $150 a day. He was just taking things out of my house selling them to get money to buy that stuff and weed I couldn't keep nothin' in my house.

– And you wrote us a letter is that right?

– Right.

– And what happened then? Tell it again. I'd just like to hear you tell it. Tell it again the way it happened after you wrote to me.

– After I wrote to you I saw a change in my son. Things started staying in my house. He started staying home. Finally he decided he's get married. Now they looking for their first chile.

– And is he off this dope thing?

– Off completely.

– And did he have to go and take a treatment?

– No, the true blue package that you been telling us about all the while – it solved my problem with God is my helper.

– God bless you God bless you. Then nobody can tell you that the True Blue Prosperity way of life isn't working for you and your son and your loved ones is that right?

— No, Reverend Franklin — everybody get that True Blue because it will make you HAPPY!

A Reversible Jacket

B. A. Merchantman is the poet in Mobile, Alabama. He meets you off the plane or the bus and he's ridiculously nice to you in the car on the way to the reading, passing you drinks and flattery and reassurance. He comes up with some line you wrote and he says how it changed his whole life one time. He tells you how his wife loves your poetry so much she wants to go to bed with you after the reading, if you can fit her in that is, because, God knows, his own students will all be there creaming their tits for you, etc.

Then comes the reading. The usual thing. You read your poems and people clap.

Now B.A. Merchantman stands up at the back of the Moon Landing Memorial Hall and says:

'Your poetry is self-orientated, Mr Blank. Do you write it for your own gratification, or do you believe, like Shelley, that poets are the legislators of the future bla bla bla?'

Well, you had your warning in the car. If you are on the ball, you say, 'Certainly. In a psychopathic world, perhaps the best place to look for new moral values is in our behaviour towards those we love, which is what I do, after a fashion.'

That's what you should have said. But it doesn't come out like that.

'But do you believe,' B.A. will be going on, 'that poetry should make itself part of the revolutionary struggle-uggle-uggle?'

'I think it's for the reader to decide whether a poem appeals to him politically,' Walter Mitty will reply.

You, on the other hand, or 'I', I should say, come up with, 'Why not?' And B.A. smiles to himself and sits down again, having proved his superior manhood.

After the reading I complimented B.A. on his fine reversible jacket.

'It isn't reversible,' he said. 'Look, I'm afraid I can't get you expenses for this reading. It seems you had to enter a claim for them in advance . . .'

I asked how I could have known what my expenses were

going to be in advance and he explained that anything would have done, $100 or more even, so long as it came in ahead of time. What they could let me have, however, if I liked, was a small 'gratuity' from an 'emergency fund' set aside for 'smash' events that had 'gone down particularly well with the students'.

'But I think we can make an exception this once,' said B.A. warmly, giving me $15 out of his wallet.

Making It Sound Like Wartime

Outside the Moon Landing Memorial Hall, where the reading had been, there was a small plaque facing the service car park:

ON THIS SITE STOOD ONE OF THE OLD
SLAVE MARKETS
Last Cargo of Slaves Arrived
On the Schooner Clotilde
In August of 1858

We got in cars and drove for a long time to the room of a Russophile journalist who made us listen to the peasant bits in a record of Prokofiev. Then it was over to the Umbrella Club, where everyone had been to a lecture on the sixties, attended by the Vice Chancellor, with an actual happening thrown in and joints handed round in a 'controlled environment' made up of silver paper and plasticine. I made a note of this as a discipline I might one day lecture in myself.

'Everything changes except the avant-garde,' I said to B.A.

'I'll have to try and catch them in Baton Rouge now,' he said regretfully.

From the Umbrella Club, various couples and a friend of B.A.'s suggested taking crayfish gumbo back to B.A.'s room on campus. This sounded like returning to GO without collecting expenses, so I suggested having a look at the town. This struck everyone as a bit weird, but we went anyway.

No one had been to the 'Moon and I' before, so we sat in a row drinking glasses of a short hot sweet fluid called White Tokay, which made everyone start jabbering at the same moment. I was sitting next to a slim and pretty primary school teacher called Jean or Joan or June, who was very embarrassed because she hadn't had time to change into evening wear.

Seeking to compliment her on her boyish figure, I tried to draw her into some mockery of a fat-bottomed woman who was leaning over the bar.

There was a slight pause, then she lit a match like a distress signal and put it to the wrong end of a cigarette, which she dropped.

'I think if I was a man,' she said eventually, 'I'd go for someone like Emmy-Lou – someone well-developed, you know? A real woman.'

I pretended not to realise that Emmy-Lou was the fat-bottom at the bar.

'There comes a point when a woman's body starts to remind you more of reproduction than sex,' I said.

'I think to a woman there's no difference between the two things.'

'You admit that there are two things then?'

'No – no.'

'You mean that when a girl lies in bed imagining a man's weight on top of her she's really thinking about having babies?'

Jane, June and Joan crossed their legs.

'I don't know,' she lied. 'A woman has to think . . . she never really knows . . . exactly *when* . . .'

Was she trying to tell me something?

'Surely today,' I said, starting to get embarrassed myself, 'I think there's proof . . . after all . . . they don't get pregnant every time . . . I don't think they're meant to . . .'

'I'll think you'll find that what most women like most about sex is just being in a man's arms . . . the warmth . . . the comradeship almost.'

'You make it sound like wartime,' I said.

'No, but a woman . . . we have to . . . trust someone . . . and that's because . . .'

Why are all Americans like Donnie and Marie Osmond?

'Listen,' I said, blundering onwards. 'You know aborigines? They don't connect . . . Before the Europeans came to Australia they didn't connect sex and birth. The tribe simply reproduced itself. Nothing interfered with the pleasures of . . .'

'Look', said Joan and everyone. 'I have to talk to Larry about tomorrow's reading. Will you excuse me?'

There was something about White Tokay which forced you to make suggestive conversation with the woman nearest to you. Left on my own, I started talking to one of the waitresses, whose name was Deborah. She told me the reason the place was empty was that The Coasters were playing down the road at The Clockwork Roadhouse. I jumped at this, but she didn't know what I meant by the ORIGINAL Coasters.

'They're called The Coasters,' she said. 'That's all I know. And they ain't those things you put your drinks on.'

When we left 'The Moon and I', it closed, so Debbie came with us to The Clockwork Roadhouse, where she seemed to be a waitress as well.

The second show was about to begin, so we had to stand at the back, where Debbie brought us a tray of White Tokay.

Of the five original Coasters only three appeared on stage, of whom one was distinctly white and the others too young to have been around much in the fifties. As if to emphasise the hazy grasp they had of their own past, they kicked off with a Drifters medley, during which Debbie told me that the Drifters were here last week and that the Platters were to follow. I wrote out my favourite Coasters tunes on a napkin and Debbie went and stood near the stage and started calling them out all wrong. 'Riot in Cellblock No. 9' came out as 'Engine Number Nahn'. She had given up being a waitress and was trying to get on stage to sing. I went for a pee and when I came back she was dancing, in what looked like a terminal fashion, with B.A. Merchantman.

Meeting Walt Whitman

The band stopped and we had more White Tokay. Then someone said they knew where we could get some Kojak. I didn't know what this meant, but I asked Debbie if she wanted to go, and of course she said yes. But first she had to pick up her son. I said I thought that would be all right and we walked down the road to a level crossing station which was lit by oil lamps and candles. Inside was an old man with a white beard and a young boy asleep on a bed.

'This is Walt Whitman,' said Debbie, introducing me to the old man. 'He's ma guardian angel.'

'How do you do, Mr Whitman,' I said. 'Are you any relation of the poet by any chance?'

There was a short silence.

'Why, Walt *is* a poet, aren't you Walt?' said Debbie.

From what I could gather, this old man's father, or grandfather, or possibly he himself, had been an acquaintance or protégé or runner of Walt Whitman's, nothing more.

'We used to go camping together over where the Model University stands today,' he told us.

'Who, you and Whitman?' I asked incredulously.

'No, me 'n granpaw,' said the old gentleman, showing us a photograph of a man on a horse. 'Granpaw used to ride fer the Pony Express. He more or less brung me up single-handed.'

'Did your grandfather ever tell you anything about the other Mr Whitman,' I asked, trying to be tactful.

My remark irritated the old fellow. It seemed he didn't take too kindly to all this confusion about the 'other' Walt Whitman.

'I dunno,' he said grumpily, 'Granpaw'd come home and find him asleep on the floor. He used to go 'bout with no clothes on or somethin', ride the horse 'n all . . .' He folded his arms, as if to put an end to the interview.

'Well, we'll be letting you get to sleep now Walt,' said Debbie, and we crept out with the sleeping child.

You Can't Clap with Kojak in Your Hand

'Where do you live?' said B.A. Merchantman, offering to give Debbie a lift home with her son.

'I taught we was going fer some Kojak,' said Debbie in surprise.

'What about Willie?'

'Willie's asleep, aren't you Willie?'

We got in the car and drove out of town to a canyon, where the lights were on in an old bungalow. June/Joan was with us and two other teacher-poets called Jim and Hogarth. Inside the bungalow a group of students were listening to someone playing the piano. He couldn't play the piano in the ordinary sense, but this wasn't affecting him in the least. He kept running his hands over the keyboard and all kinds of modern sounds were shooting out of it. He got up and someone else who couldn't play sat down.

With some difficulty, the owner of the bungalow poured me a glass of this Kojak and I soon realised that everyone in the room was drunk, including me. By the time I had taken a second glass I was playing the piano myself. I was like Sparky running amazed hands over his magic keyboard. 'I've always wanted to play an instrument,' I thought to myself. 'Now I'm doing it!'

'You play very well for a beginner,' slurred the owner.

'It's easier than it looks,' I said when I was forced to stop due to finger-cramp.

'When you've been playing all evening, like Hoss 'n myself, you get to be able to play almost anything . . .'

The next time the piano was free we sat down and played a duet together. Vic was the perfect foil to my invention. Jim and Hogarth, who were in the college orchestra, said they had to phone their wives. Since there wasn't a phone on the premises they set out down the dark canyon and were never seen again.

'I can sing a song,' said Debbie.

'Sing one then.'

'O you can't clap with Kojak in you hand,' sang
  Debbie,
'But you can whistle you way across the land
Pickin and grinning and having fun
Drinkin moonshine, not getting much done.
O I haven't learned much in this rock 'n roll band
But I know you can't clap with Kojak in your hand.'

This was thought to be a great triumph and as a reward B.A. Merchantman agreed to dance with Debbie, who then began hopping all over the small cabin. Out of politeness I asked June if she would like to dance, hoping she would refuse, since I wanted to play the piano again. June had had a slug of Kojak herself. She not only wanted to dance, she wanted to hug. We were soon necking in the back of B.A.'s car, where I had the confusing impression that June's light-as-air body was flying around my head like a moth. I was so drunk I couldn't remember in what sequence you progress at times like this. Our love-making, if you can call it that, was like an avant-garde play, having no beginning or end, but a longish middle section, during which we were interrupted by Debbie and Willie, who wanted to go home.

It seemed that Debbie was furious with B.A. because he had tried to get her to stop singing.

'I know who you are B.A. Merchantman,' she was saying all

the way to her home on the far side of town. 'I know you're a married man and you work at the Model University. I can soon find your address you know, so don't think you can insult me like that in front of everyone and get away with it.' The poor girl was in floods of drunken tears.

'Here,' said B.A., taking a handful of dollars out of his wallet. 'For God's sake. I'm sorry. Buy yourself some flowers.'

I was surprised to see that this seemed to pacify Debbie, who then gave him her telephone number. I couldn't help wondering whether Debbie's gratuity had come out of B.A.'s own pocket, or, like mine, from the Emergency Fund set up to deal with events that had 'gone down particularly well with the students'.

5
THE SOUTHERN ROUTE WEST

Thom Gunn? You Wrote 'Elvis Presley'

The last time I saw Thom Gunn was in the Hope & Anchor in London. I'd persuaded him to come and see my friends Dr Feelgood play in this Islington cellar and I dragged him into the dressing room afterwards. Wilko Johnson was impressed, but Lee Brilleaux said, 'Thom Gunn? You wrote "Elvis Presley"'. We had to learn that at school.' And he recited it for us. Thom later referred to the band as 'shameless'.

I never had to learn Thom Gunn at school. I came upon him by chance in the *New Lines* anthology I got out of the County Library. His sensible toughness was the perfect antidote to adolescence and I bought an unwearable (then) black leather jacket as soon as possible – 'Heard, as he stretched back from his beer/Leather creak softly round his neck and chin'. It creaked far from softly round my skinny neck, but I was still wearing it – sleeve ripped and much scarred – when I arrived in America for the first time twenty years later. One of the things I most wanted to do there was visit Thom in San Francisco, the place he had vanished to when I was still at school.

The other was to visit April Stanley. April was actually the main reason I went to America in the first place, thinking there'd be others like her there, which there weren't. I'd met her in Paris a few years earlier when she was working as a courier-cum-model (warm as one, cool as the other) and I'd never forgotten her or her address in LA.

A Holiday Area

A dead-looking, man-made beach stretches the length of the State of Mississippi. The dry, pale sand looks like it's made of the bones of all the hikers and bikers and trikers, itinerant prostitutes and tourist-beaters who drift back and forth along the Gulf coast between Florida and New Orleans. Every now and then there is a sad little outcrop of palm trees with a flag proclaiming it a 'Holiday Area'. But the trees have struck rock. Their trunks bow this way and that, lifting tired roots to the hot, flinty wind. Only the vast hoarding to Newport Cigarettes — 'LOW TAR WITH THAT TANG OF MOUNTAIN AIR' — remains upright, like some mad sailing ship out on the dusty dunes.

We're coming into Pascagoula now: SHOE CITY. The bus calls like a taxi at Moody's Motel and a young priest waves goodbye to his girlfriend. The Holy Cross Bookstore has a crooked cross dangling by a wire from the roof. This is Baptist territory: all over the South these church-cum-clubs are for the white-minded ultra-conservative middle classes only, with no drinking, smoking or dancing permitted (or desired). Full immersion baptism is the only thing they share with the black, downtown, Martin Luther King section, known as the Holy Rollers, who do lots of everything.

A fat boy in the Estabrook Greyhound sub-station reminds me of what work looks like: he piles the parcels for despatch on to a small trolley, small ones first, since they come first, then the big flat ones on top. He moves so slowly between the parcels shed and the trolley that at first nothing happens. Then they all slither into an oily patch near the wheel of one of the coaches. The fat boy, who has a straggly ginger moustache, looks at the mess, then goes back into the shade of the parcels office to fiddle with labels for the rest of his life.

A Lovely Location Spot

Sky, sea and sand at Biloxi are three different shades of fawn. It looks like a bad painting of a desert, with a single nodding-donkey oil well for mirage. I note that LOANS UNLIMITED are available to HAPPY FAMILIES & OTHERS, but that nice guy from Minnesota should never have moved all the way down here, even if he was in love with a Mississippi girl. Pleasure Boating on Emerald Lake looks like a trip to the end of the world. They say that this lighthouse was painted black when Lincoln was assassinated, but now it's in mourning for Biloxi. Humpty's Dump serves the Masonic Temple.

Before the war, motels were called Tourist Courts. Now the word 'motel' has got a bad name, due to *Psycho* and other films, so the fashion is for Motor Hotels. I see the Sun 'n Sand Motor Lodge has Seafood-in-the-Rough, but there's only time for a Hershey Bar unfortunately.

Immobile figures, knee-deep in stagnant Gulf water, wave to the bus at Gulf Port. This is Ocean Wave Avenue, with Breath's Real Estate advertised, but no wrinkle on the wooden sea. A station wagon full of children drives out on to the beach to where the swings stand like scaffolds against the brown horizon. Why are we driving into the Divine World Seminary? It seems the great Greyhound Bus Co. becomes a local service in places. Diana's Country Kitchen has hard and soft crabs from Lake Catherine . . , but on we go. I throw my Hershey wrapper in a trash can in the shape of a seagull.

As we enter Louisiana, Mr Kay, my neighbour, points to the little houses stuck on stilts over the reeds, each with its own jetty.

'How sweet it is,' he observes. 'A lovely location spot.'

This is my cue, but I try not to ask him if he is in films.

'When I was in films . . .' he begins.

Baton Rouge, Opelousas, the bayous with the their bearded oaks petering out towards Texas. Paddy fields in full green, a child on a little postcard Palomino canters along with us for a moment.

'Texas is ugly and flat, like Texas women,' observes Mr Kay. I haven't had a square meal since Alabama. I should have got something in Baton Rouge, but I couldn't cash a cheque.

A Phase He's Going Through

At Lake Charles I jump out and walk five blocks to the bank. The cashier looks a long time at my traveller's cheque and says slowly:

'Are you the author?'

I say I am a writer, hoping there is another one for him to be thinking of, but he shows me a photo of his son, who came to a course I took on Dylan Thomas in London in 1977.

'He's never been the same since that trip to Europe,' says the man. 'He went to a monastery, I don't know if you knew, after that course of yours. He told us he'd changed. We didn't know how much.'

'He seemed quiet, you know?' I suggest, vaguely remembering someone showing an interest in drugs.

'He didn't say anything to you about the Miroku Bosatsu did he?' says the man.

'He was reading Freud and things. I think he had a poem about a rock . . .'

'His girlfriend says he's completely passive nowadays.'

'Perhaps it's just a phase he's going through?'

'He shaved all his head. We don't know what's gotten into him. Listen, mister, I sure would welcome the chance to discuss him with you, if you have the time that is . . .'

I begin to see my hot chicken dinner vanishing from sight once more, and the bus, with my luggage on board, leaving without me.

'He just sits in his room all day playing the flute. He says his name is Miroku Bosatsu. I sure wish you'd talk to him, mister.'

'Listen,' I tell the man, 'why don't you give me your address . . . ?'

The man hands me my hundred dollars, which he clearly thinks I don't deserve. I grab it and race the five blocks to my bus, which is about to leave. I scramble in and find that Mr Kay has got the window seat. He has had time for 'a fine little snack' he tells me. The taco was 'excellent, with good sauce', his only complaint being that the lettuce was not finely enough chopped. Again, the rice was not well liked. 'It needs work,' he tells me, savouring the remains of his meal as it comes up on his breath.

'It's a touchy question, chicken,' he begins again, just as I have started to forget my hunger. 'It's the number one problem for any chicken chain, you know. Is it a white product, or is it a black product? That's the question. They have to make their minds up on that point, then go ahead and present it one way or the other. It's no use sitting on the fence . . .'

'Sabine Orange the lake fer Arthur and the Nederlands,' hollers B.F. Kent, our 'operator', who like all 'operators' is SAFE RELIABLE COURTEOUS, though I still can't understand what he says when he announces places. You have to jump out and look on the back of a postcard, otherwise all you see is FUN TOWN SKIN TRIALS, SULPHUR BEEF SHOT or something, which leaves you ignorant and alone: a common state for travellers.

The bus has San Francisco on the front and I'm tempted to go all the way – three days and two nights on my neck. The thing is you have to be organised – get enough to eat and drink, then you can sleep all right. Now my sore throat's coming back: I'll get out my leather jacket.

It seems that that was the Sabine river, the Texas State Line, the one Janis Joplin used to roar across with the boys from Port Arthur, looking for rough times in the riverside bars on the Louisiana side. Janis used to pick fights with the lowlife characters over there and her men friends would have trouble getting back to decent Texas alive.

Mr Kay seems to have vanished. In his place is a little drunk man in a neat red suit.

'Houston is the fastest growing city in the world,' he tells me aggressively. 'It's bigger than Japan. For a simple person like me, a place like Houston, well, it has everything – alligators in the zoo, modern streets. Of course,' he looks modest suddenly, so that I feel he is slightly mad, 'it's still very difficult to break into the acting and singing professions. Me? Nah, I'm in collection and dispersal systems, ha ha ha!'

We experience twenty-five miles of urban sprawl coming into this fine modern place. Only LOVE WIGS and a building which uses scaffolding as a part of the design relieve the oppressive monotony.

'It looks somewhat depressing from here,' I say.

'Yes, Houston has everything if you're willing to look for it.'

We enter the bus station concourse together and Davy stands on a seat and tries to get me to come up beside him. 'Look,' he says, pointing at someone on the far side of the hall, 'you see that little bitch over there . . .'

'Yes.'

'Sodding off to Dallas I dare say.'

'How do you know?'

'They're all the same in Dallas. Look . . . see that other one? The one in the hat? Crippled! Too nervous! Ugh!' He nearly falls off the seat in his disgust and I have to steady him. Noting his interest in the opposite sex, I ask him if there are any clubs or dance halls in Houston.

'Dancing? No, I don't think so, not in Houston. They got rid of all that kind of crap for the elections. Shifted it over to the swamp area. Now you gotta get your arse in a taxi, regular clean-up job, course it all creeps back in the end, but they don't think of that. Me? Nah, I'm just here to sober up before I get home.'

I decide to have a wash and clean-up. When I come out Davy runs over to me and says we're going out with two girls tonight, quick, what's my name, he wants me to meet Ally-May and Cora.

'But I'm catching the bus tonight . . .'

'Catch it tomorrow. Tonight we're staying at the William Penn Hotel with Ally-May and Cora.'

We hurry over to the hotel, where the two girls are said to be dying to meet me. On the way up in the lift a big black man starts complaining about losing a horseshoe diamond ring.

'I been sleeping in this hotel non-stop fer nahn years,' he moans. 'I drive trucks. I drive em hard. I's respectable. One horseshoe diamond. How d'you like that?'

I check my watch and realise I've left it in the Greyhound washroom. I tear back there, but it's gone. 'Ya shouldna go leavin' ya ting on a slab fer black fella niggra ta filch fer ya . . .' the black warder tells me.

Back at the William Penn, Davy is beside himself with anxiety. Cora has been there and left again, finding him alone. Davy says it is my fault that we are booked into a two-star hotel and no broads. I buy him one or two drinks and we contemplate investigating the Purple Massage Studio opposite the bus station, since this seems to be the one and only corner of excitement in sanitised downtown Houston.

Film Stars and Dogs

Inside this falling-down shack is a row of multi-coloured masseuses. Davy can't make up his mind which one he likes best, so he says he'd like to think about it. I was going to say the same thing myself, but don't feel I can now. I choose the one who looks at me hardest and follow her down a passage. She is mostly black, with big grey eyes. She has on yellow shorts and a T-shirt. We go into a small room papered with film stars and dogs. There is an easy chair and a chamber pot, which the girl sits on.

'You wanna drink?' she says. 'Take off your pants.'

Obviously zero per cent of customers are looking for a genuine massage, so the question never arises. What *is* being offered seems unclear. I get undressed.

'Name's Ricky,' says the girl, sitting down on my lap. 'Whassamatter? This your first time with a girl?'

'No. Nothing's the matter,' I gulp.

She begins rubbing my shoulders and whispering something I don't understand. Then she gets astride my lap and I hold her waist.

'I suppose you want this off,' she says, taking off her T-shirt.

'Take your shorts off,' I suggest.

'Hey-Hey-Hey,' says Ricky, smacking me across the mouth. 'This is a legitimate studio, you know. What you think I am?'

She gets up and goes over to a box. I think at first that she has a gun, but it turns out to be an old-fashioned vibro-massage.

'Put this on,' she says, handing me a rubber.

A minute later the vibro-pad has produced an involuntary semi-ejaculation, which at first I don't recognise as such. Ricky does, however. She takes the rubber, ties a knot in it and flings it into a fireplace full of orange peel.

'Have a good time honey?'

Next morning I met up with Davy and asked him how he got on.

'Me?' he said. 'Nah, didn't fancy it. Tracked down old Ally-May at the depot. She 'n Cora was with this trucky. I give her twenty dollars and she come back with me. We're going to Dallas. Ally-May's in the removals trade, ha ha ha. She got this big old semi . . .'

'What happened to Cora?'

'I told her you'd gone over the massage studio for a moment and she sloped off with the man behind the bar. Said for her to wait and everything, but . . . you know . . . these Dallas girls . . . they don't care what they do . . .'

Sky lowering over Sandy Fork Creek outside Houston. 'Your operator: A.M. MINNIE-WEATHER – SAFE RELIABLE COURTEOUS.' The western-style gentleman sitting next to me has on a smart brown cowboy suit, very pointed tan boots and a little lopped-off brown silk tie with a tiny saxophone hanging from it. He is a handsome man of sixty or more.

'I was in San Pedro California this time last March,' he tells the rainy window.

'What took you to San Pedro?'

'A fee-male,' he says inscrutably, turning intense periwinkle blue eyes in my direction.

'How long you stay?'

'Two whole days I stayed in San Pedro . . .'

'It didn't work out then?'

He shakes his head as if to put an end to some unwelcome noise in his brain.

'Have some gum,' I say.

'Thank-you. I believe I will at that!'

He sits forward in his seat like a boy.

'Gee Whiz,' he says suddenly, 'will you take a look at that PECAN! If that ain't one mutherfuckin pee-can!'

Outside Seguin Town Hall is a notice board with gold lettering:

SEGUIN. HOME OF THE WORLD'S LARGEST PECAN

In front of it, on a fine pedestal, is a statue of a yard-long, foot-high pecan nut.

'Next stop will be San Anton,' says A.M. Minnie-Weather happily.

The westerner covers his mouth with his hand. 'That's because there ain't a blamed thing tween here and thar savin the Alamo Fireworks,' he cackles.

'I Was Eating Eggs in Sammy's Place When a Black Man Drew His Knife'

'San Antonio,' said the man in This Is It Café, surveying his birthplace pessimistically, 'San Antonio's a great place to be from, if you take my meaning. You got somewhere better to go you get your arse the hell outta San Antonio. I been home two years, I never looked out the window one time. What's to see?'

I watched a straggle of sombreroed sleepwalkers gather round a hole in the wall selling enchaladas.

'The conditioner breaks down you make it to the phone. That's an EVENT. The boy comes round this week you're in luck. Listen. How many songs you hear about San Antonio?'

'I don't know . . .'

'I'll tell you. A whole bunch. And fer why? They got out! Why does a man write a song about a place? Because he knows deep down he ain't never going back. No, you wanna see the world you get your arse to Houston, boy.'

'HOUSTON?'

'Sure. You know what they say about Houston? They say when Texas breaks clear of the Union Houston's gonna be the Number One town in North America. And that means the world.'

'Why not Dallas?'

'Dallas? Dallas got too many fucking niggers, if you take my meaning. Now don't get me wrong. I ain't prejudiced. Not like some of the folks around here. I'm jus telling you the facts. You take my advice you'll head on over to Houston. That's the place for a young fella like yourself . . .'

The man put his stetson on his head and stepped out into the sun.

Almost Heaven Peanut Butter

From the window of the bus we take in The Melody Club, Talk of the Town Carwash, All Right Car Sales, Happy World Laundry. But if you could see the background of Kerrsville, Texas, you would marvel at these things. For here is your classic strung-out township: dusty, provincial, drab. A great place to be *from*, as they say. Only its names, with their forlorn glamour, seem to rise above it all, as if they sprang from some lost happiness. Look at that lawn-mower shop, The Garden of Eden. On the outskirts of the town, dwarfed by a water tower, surrounded by an oil slick, is the Hollywood Cocktail Lounge, a one-storey establishment which falls away to hardly more than a lean-to behind its burnt-wood façade painted with champagne bubbles.

Travelling around America I am struck by the very loose relationship the place has with its language. It's like pornography, where the simple facts tend to get conceptualised out of all recognition by inflationary wish-fulfilment. Thus, it is a simple matter for a shop to become a store, a store to become a mart, a mart to become a centre, a centre to become a 'world' and a world to become a 'dream'. I have yet to see a Wet Dream Trailer Park, though there are plenty of Climax Snack Bars, a pop group called The Comers and a brand of peanut butter called 'Almost Heaven'.

The Era Has Long Passed

More and more grey-green fields with stunted oaks, the world so flat a slight gradient is called Mount Prospero and has a dollar sign branded on it. Now Fort Lancaster has a table mountain. I saw two wild mustangs with white manes and tails. All this is supposed to be western terrain (Lone Star Beer, High Noon Trailer Park) but there is no feeling of anything at all unless it is the map of America being drawn past one's eyes.

'You drive and drive and you're still in Texas tomorrow night,' said Dean Moriarty.

'In regard to admitting thousands of Vietnamese boat people to this country,' begins the letter in the *San Angelo Standard Times* ('The Good Morning Paper For The Golden West of Texas'), 'I think the era has long passed when we should welcome all the oppressed and downtrodden people to our shores . . .' What makes him think this is a country, I wonder?

Dusk comes down quickly and I see an owl sitting in the one shrub for miles. Windmills laid out like pylons in long lines, the see-saw oil-wells look like bending Dutch land-girls in white hats and pants. I see a burning bush far off but it is only a maverick oil flare, smell of oil in the air and ash floating down.

Tomms Corn-Cheez, Adam's Artificial Sour Grape Flavouring, Joe's Pecan Brownies, but what's the name of the town? At American Parts they stack cars on their noses like fish. I jump down and send cards to everyone I'm missing from some hot greasy place I don't know the name of and you can't ask really. When I asked for a can of drink they said crossly, 'The drink's in cups,' and I stood in the doorway looking a hundred miles west to the sunset sending its last beams shooting between the wheels of the bus, lighting the ground at my feet from the side like a relief.

I read that 'Ten United Farm Workers Union sympathisers were wounded Monday when a South Texas melon farmer said he "opened season" on them with an automatic shotgun. The farmer said "They were carrying those red flags. They'll be easy to recognise. The leader ran at me with a club. I shot him full-face with my shot-gun." He said the union demonstrators were trampling his melons and trying to get his workers to leave the melon fields.'

On the road to El Paso the bus is filled with glamorous pink light like a nightclub and talk starts up about the sudden sunset and the cold. Pink lightning flickers like a country electricity supply over the huge plain. The table-top mountains have withdrawn to a backdrop, lit by purple mist which floats just above the horse-scrub. Now a rainstorm edges towards us, as if a child was shading it in with a pencil.

The Set-Up

I was supposed to reach Armandias College, El Paso, this time last year, but I couldn't get enough readings together, so cancelled the trip. I'd written two hundred letters to colleges all over the States, but most of them said the money had been allocated for that year and to try again next year. You have to get to them at least eighteen months in advance, otherwise the funds have been snapped up by the lecturer in Dunlopillo and the Belly Dancing Club. A friend of mine tours America almost constantly, lecturing on, and committing, 'Adultery'. Another reads out his thesis on 'The Blurb'. I heard of a man who got $35,000 from the government for a single talk on Clearasil. But that's all up-market stuff. Poetry is so far down market they have to pump air back to it. I realised later that the gimmick is to say, 'I'm planning to be in your area,' then the college secretaries relax a little and you plan your itinerary accordingly.

Anyway, I had sent fifty copies of my book to El Paso in advance, meaning to take them on to California afterwards. Determined to get hold of them now, I rang Professor Flower, my contact in Literature. A stage Mexican answered the phone and said Señor Flower was in the Yemen, why not I don't try

Señor Gomez in Conservation? I rang Señor Gomez and what
sounded like the same person answered the phone and said he
would meet me outside the Nueces Chilli-Bar in an hour.

The Look-See Man

Tired from hunger and hungry from lack of sleep, I wandered
in and out of the Greyhound Souvenir Shop, mistaking
the brightly coloured symbols for something that might sustain
or satisfy me. The same knick-knacks, with different names
touched in, do duty as souvenirs all over America: the ashtray
like a saddle, the paper-rack in the form of a ranch. On many a
meaningless meander I have stood anxiously before these
tokens, checked the Empire State Building thermometer,
nearly bought the buffalo tie-slide, the six-shooter earrings,
priced the drum majorette nutcrackers. Now I was so softened
up by the great Texas scrubscape that I found myself combing
the rack of 3D postcards for sustenance. In vain I chose between galleons, mustangs, the Last Supper, stalactites, a shoot-
out, parrots, tigers, lovers. The Last Supper seemed appealing.
I had just found a whole pile of black and white pictures of
Juarez, across the border, when a smooth little Mexican
touched my hand and said that the shoot-out was 'pretty neat'.
I bought that one to satisfy him and escaped into the rest room.

I shouldn't have encouraged him. I heard someone jangling
change behind me and glancing over my shoulder, saw the little
Mexican, his eyes ablaze for a shoot-out. He was soon next to
me, standing on tip-toe in order to peer over the partition, an
expression of haughty machismo on his taut features. I gave up
and went to wait in the Nueces Chilli-Bar.

The Meet

Doctor Gomez reminded me of the man in the rest room: short,
glossy and camp. We went to his place and drank tequila. The
doctor got out of his maroon velvet jacket and put on a crested
blazer. He was editing an anthology of unconventional love
poetry for the University of Texas, he told me, clinking my
glass.

'Unconventional?' I asked.

'Esoteric . . . you know, *sophisticated* . . . ?'

'Oh I get it.'

'I was wondering whether you'd ever tried anything like that?'

'There might be one in my book . . . I never can learn my work by heart.'

'Well, why don't we ask Forbes if he knows where they are?'

Obviously Gomez had only the haziest insight or interest in the location of my books, but Forbes put on the lights in Old Books and Gomez showed me a first edition of an unconventional American novel. We searched in Manuscripts and Periodicals and Literature and then Forbes said he remembered when it was all a desert out here, implying that it had been easier to find things in those days.

'I think the best thing for you to do,' he said hopelessly, 'is to ask Mrs Knott. She knows all there is to know about Armandias.'

'A sensible idea', said Gomez, 'and now, if you will excuse me . . . ?'

His tightly waisted blazer disappeared in the direction of the bus station.

The Woman

Mrs Knott was a plump, fanciable housewife in a string of pearls: a sadist's paradise. We met in the Post House Drug Store. She took my hand and said she wanted to hear all about the Arts in London, with special reference to Theatre. A bit of give-and-take, in other words.

All my life I have loved having a famous actor for a father. No occasion, first term at school included, had been inauspicious enough for me to keep my mouth shut on the subject. As soon as I had told Mrs Knott that my father had been in *David Copperfield* and *Wuthering Heights* and that he was an old friend of Laurence Olivier, I knew I had set back my own best interests by several hours. She asked me was I sure about these things, then she ran to the phone to tell Peggy. Peggy was at work, but she came running over with her autograph book expecting to find Laurence Olivier, or, at the very least some film star friend of his sitting in the soda bar. There was a cheated look in her eye when she learned the truth and she had a little row with Mrs Knott, disguised as a discussion about banana cake. She took my signature all the same, at the back of her book, and said I was to give a talk to the Drama Club. Then it was back to her place to see her Drama Awards, one of which had been presented by Mickey Rooney.

'Mickey sat right there in that chair you're sitting in,' she said grudgingly. I bounced up and down a little to show my appreciation. Then I asked if anyone had any idea where my fifty books might have got to. Mrs Knott said they were certainly in the Senior Quiet Room, so we had some banana cake, then we went over there.

The Find

The Senior Quiet Room was locked. Forbes was sent for. He'd been asleep. He said crossly that he'd seen *Wuthering Heights* as a boy but couldn't remember my father. He let us in and went back to his cubby-hole. The Senior Quiet Room had thick white carpets and Mexican wallhangings. No books anywhere. I felt like a quick kip on one of the white leather Chesterfields, but Mrs Knott had the bit between her teeth by this time.

'We'll just check the College Bookstore,' she said craftily.

At the bookshop a Mr Spitz said his wife Helen was asleep upstairs right now, but if we'd care to look around for ourselves, not making too much noise, we were very welcome. I found the books before he had finished speaking, clearly visible beside his left boot. They were where all authors beginning with 'w' are located: on the shelf by the floor. There were thirty-six of them, marked at $4 each. Mr Spitz had no immediate explanation for this. He couldn't say anything without asking his wife, he said. Perhaps I would like to come back in the morning?

Miguel Puts In the Symbols

I stayed the night with Mr and Mrs Knott and in the morning I went over to the bookshop to find out how my books had turned up there. I was determined to come away with either the copies or the money for them. Mrs Spitz was still absent, but Mr Spitz greeted me warmly.

'I like your poems,' he said, 'I like them a lot. So did Helen. You've got talent.'

'Thank you,' I said.

'Poems like that, I can't understand it. They should have gone OK. You're problem's production . . .'

'Really?'

'Sure. Look at your jacket. "Don't buy me" written all over it.'

'I like the way it looks.'

'Listen before you leave El Paso I'd like to show you something. Helen . . .' He called up the stairs to his wife, 'Is it OK if I show Mr Williams round the studio?'

There was no answer, so Mr Spitz led the way down some stairs, unlocked a small door and showed me into a brightly lit office where half a dozen people were bent over drawing boards.

'This is planning and production,' said Mr Spitz. 'The nerve centre of our operation.'

I noticed the little Mexican from the bus station rest room. He waved to me and mouthed a silent 'Hi!'

'I see you two have met,' said Mr Spitz. 'Miguel's one of our most talented contributors. He came to Planning via Ceramics. Now he writes full-time . . .'

'Writes?'

'Sure. Didn't I tell you? This whole building is a creative powerhouse. We export all over the world. The bookshop's only a sideline. Some people call it a front, ha ha ha!'

'Export what?' I asked.

'Oh, posters, diaries, calendars, cards, pendants, bookmarks, anthologies, you name it. This is a full-scale production unit.'

'Posters? Of what?'

'Thoughts, you know, poems, inspirations, poetry mostly . . .'

'Miguel writes them?'

'Not exactly. Miguel puts in the symbols. They're all traditional. He has this incredible instinct for the right image. We call him Michael Angelo . . .'

The talented Miguel was standing in front of me, saying nothing, but beaming proudly and jingling the change in the pocket of his flared trousers.

'You know, the more I think about that book of yours,' said Mr Spitz, 'the more I think there might be something we could do to redeem the situation . . .'

'How do you mean?'

'Tell me something. How many copies you sell? Ten thousand?'

'Nothing like.'

'Every item we produce here sells over a hundred thousand a year or we wouldn't produce it. I don't know how Helen would feel about this, but I was going to suggest you collaborated with Miguel here.'

'Collaborate?'

'Sure. Rough something out with Miguel. That lullaby of yours for instance. Then we'll pass it on to Ramon, see what he can come up with. Antonio could take care of the background.'

As if to prove his prowess, Miguel showed me one of his latest creations, a keyring with the legend 'The Pleasures Of This World Shall Pass Away But My Words Shall Not Pass Away' printed on a little tablet with a background of reeds, which seemed to be slipping off the top of the tablet.

'Production problem,' said Miguel, as he tried to show me how the keyring might fit into my pocket.

'You could say that Miguel was in charge of quality control,' laughed Mr Spitz, 'whereas Ramon here monitors emotional response. Something like that anyway. Ramon was born on the border, weren't you Ramon?'

'Señor?'

'It's all very informal here. We enjoy our work. It's a modest operation, but these boys have such a feeling for natural poetry, natural philosophy. Sometimes I get quite sentimental about them. They're so *talented*. Take a look at this.'

He showed me a cream-coloured poster with a background of rain-clouds:

> Our love is like the sky
> It covers us like a blanket
> When it is sunny we smile
> When it rains we cry
> The stars come out when we kiss
> Sometimes there is thunder in the sky
> That is only natural
> The lightning shows us how small we are
> Compared to the sky of our love

'I believe that's some of Ramon's work, isn't it Ramon?' said Mr Spitz.

Ramon bridled with pleasure at the mention of his work.

'Ramon hasn't been to Business College like Miguel. He never even heard the Great American Lie, did you Ramon?'

Ramon stuck out a long tongue and giggled shyly behind another Mexican, who gave him a push.

'I used to be in business myself until I met Helen,' said Mr Spitz, 'but she showed me where my head was at.'

'You're not doing so badly,' I said.

'Helen learnt everything she knows from Rodrigo. Then I picked up what I could from Helen.'

'Who's Rodrigo?'

'Rodrigo? Rodrigo's getting on a bit now. He's not here all the time, but he still shows people round the University. He even wrote the brochure.'

'Is he here today?'

'Sure. He's through here in leatherwork . . . Rodrigo, I'd like you to meet Mr Williams . . . Mr Williams is an . . . er . . . writer . . . also . . .'

'I am pleased to meet you,' said Rodrigo. 'You will buy my book of the University?'

The old man found a copy of the pamphlet and waited for me to pay him. It was illustrated with rough pictures of cacti and haciendas, surrounded by patches of yellow and red.

'Let him have one free, Rodrigo,' said Mr Spitz, 'he might be working with Miguel . . .'

'About this idea,' I said, 'I'm supposed to be leaving El Paso tonight . . . I don't know . . . If you wanted to use something out of the book . . . I suppose . . .'

'No problem,' said Mr Spitz. 'You have this lullaby poem, right?'

'Right.'

'That's exactly what we want. Now what Helen had in mind was this. Silkscreen your poem on to pillowcases for the teenage market. Part of it anyway.'

'Part of the teenage market?'

'Part of the poem.'

'I see . . .'

'What do you say?'

'I say how much.'

'How MUCH? Well, we'll use your name, naturally, but we can't hold out any financial incentive just now. As you know, the household market is a highly competitive area and . . .'

'Incidentally, I was hoping to find out how my books came to be on your shelves in the first place.'

'Look. Does it MATTER? HONESTLY? You know, I understand how you feel. I've been in your shoes. At heart, Helen and I are just a couple of old hippies who struck lucky. We'd still be back in St Louis smoking pot if it hadn't been for Rodrigo.'

'Good old Rodrigo!'

'You know what he taught us?'

'No.'

'Turn yourself to face the world. That's what he said.'

'I thought that was David Bowie . . .'

'Well, anyway, this year we bought the film rights to *The Prophet*.'

'There's one thing I can't understand about all this. Do you believe in all this crap, or are you totally cynical about it?'

'Let me ask you a question in return, my friend. Do you believe in this vase of flowers? Or are you cynical about it?'

'I'm cynical about it.'

'That's what I was afraid of.'

'No need to be afraid.'

'And you know something else? That's the reason your poetry doesn't sell.'

De Mark of de Debil

On the bus that night, I dream I'm visiting a film set of *The Prophet*, where my brother is living on a raft. He's building his own flat there: leaves and children. The nurse shows me where her room will be, winking wildly. I thank her, but have to apologise for the way my neck keeps flopping over, until it snaps upright and I see we are in Deming, New Mexico.

'Ah've come to de conclusion', says the travelling black lady sitting next to me, 'dat our sunset is other fella's sunrise. Dat's how we get de difference in de hours.'

'You're right,' I tell her, 'but it comes to an end in California. That's where Western Time has to turn round and head east again.'

'Sho does,' says the black lady. 'Ah've wrassled in Florida,

Hawaii and de Grand Canyon, but ah prefer de Florida any day.'

Next she has something to whisper to me about the unfortunate man sitting behind us, who has a birthmark running down his face, that it's 'de mark of de debil'.

'How's that for an express ride?' says the driver as we pull up in the empty stillness of some early morning township and get down like the ghosts of a chain gang to look for our sustenance in the morgue-like, mauve-upholstered House of Standlock, Ellis S. Brown, Your Host.

In the rest room of this depopulated terminal there is a bright dispenser for prophylactics that are 'so different, so exciting', which makes me wonder how different a prophylactic can be and still be exciting. Either way, they seem to have been a success in Lordsburg, New Mexico, which is a ghost town.

I buy a postcard of 'Indian Sheepherders Trekking Across The Brilliant Sands Of Monument Valley, Arizona, As Seen From The Panoramic Windows Of A High-Level Air-Conditioned Trailways Silver Eagle Bus'. Then it is time to get back on board.

'My friend never did like de geography or de history,' observes my neighbour, nodding at a heap of bones lying in the desert. 'She used to cut out all de things she liked and stick dem in her book.'

The landscape has turned to blown dust, teeth mountains in the distance. I open a copy of the *Texas Spokesman* and read of Ronald O'Bryan, a thirty-year-old Houston optician who was sentenced to death in the electric chair for murdering his eight-year-old son to collect on life insurance. The Houston jury of ten men and two women deliberated an hour and eleven minutes before returning the death sentence.

Back to Dreamland

Night juggernauts plough past, the railroad drills to our right. My thoughts have been left behind by this westwardness, but I must keep up with the bus. I hold the pony's mane and trot in my sleep like a defeated brave. It's the Arizona state line and a policeman is beside me asking if I have any grapefruit or orange juice. I pull myself together, imagining he is thirsty.

'No boy, I don't wanna drink. Go back to dreamland.'

Going through Bowie we see Geronimo's Castle, a concrete teepee. Indians slouch in the doorway of WIG-O-RAMA which 'Puts The Fun Back Into Top-Knots'. At the drive-in, *The Thing* is 'AMAZING BUT TRUE'. 'Don't Feel Like a Stranger,' a bank tells me, 'GET THE ARIZONA KIT'. Through the gap in the seats I watch in irritation as two love-birds peck incessantly at one another. In Phoenix I feel like the man with the block of ice I see standing at the entrance to another Miracle Mile: Karate Parlours, brake shops, motor banks, Jack-in-the-box burgers, Quartzite and Gold Nugget Roads, Apache Boulevard, 'Old Folks! Come to Youngtown!', 'RAIN FOR RENT'. At the edge of town the giant cacti satirise us in slow-motion semaphore: why dash to nothingness? At last the cry goes up: 'CALIFORNIA!' Now it all makes sense.

Like Peeling Off a Glove

At Blythe, California, Oasis and Marina, some orthodox Jews are standing near a station wagon with their feet together. So far the Promised Land looks like the rest of America. It's still scrubby and dry-looking, but it has more garages. Now one of the orthodox Jews begins bowing jerkily and saying something to himself, one hand touching the station wagon. A smaller, fatter one, with red side-locks, blows a bubble, interrupting his father's prayer. I believe they are seeing someone off on our bus. Yes, a pretty daughter in ordinary clothes is getting on to the bus. She sits down next to me and says her name is Anne Osterlitz. Her brother plays lead guitar with Anaconda, who sometimes support the Doobie Brothers. To back this claim she brings out a little joint, which we smoke. She is full of life, leaving home for the first time to make her name in films. Her hero is Jack Nicholson and she's going straight to his house. We go through a field of cacti and Anne tells me that they attack you if you come to within a foot of them. Can this be right?

Our conversation subsides because a man close behind is describing in full detail, to a pale man in glasses, how to trap, skin, clean and stretch some unnamed mammal, possibly a musk-rat. I can't see the speaker, but he has an aggressive, high-pitched voice which keeps breaking. He seems irritated about something and says everything is a 'cinch', especially the gutting. I get the impression he would like to take his hunting

knife to his companion, who can only offer the occasional
'Right' when told how you just rip the rat's coat inside out from
ear to toe. 'It's a cinch,' he says, his voice cracking with
violence, 'like peeling off a glove.' His companion leans past my
head to wind down the window. Thanks to these two, Anne and
I exchange loving looks.

Midnight and Bakersfield

Smoke trees at Indio shade the desert into vineyard and orange
groves. To the left, white sand. To the right, sharp mountains
in relief. I don't want to strain my eyes uselessly, but girls in
cars we pass seem noticeably more glamorous than of late.
Without looking away from the window I lay my hand on
Anne's lap, palm upwards.

'Anaconda got all the groupies they can handle,' she tells me,
tickling it with her finger. 'The Doobies aren't into groupies.
Really beautiful girls, you know? They're mad, don't you
think? Rob tells me everything.'

'What kind of thing?'

'He took me to this pyramid party in Bel-Air. Everyone took
their clothes off. It was crazy, but I left my glasses behind. We
were in this big pyramid . . .'

'Did the men stay sharp, like razor-blades?'

'Everyone was taking acid. I wasn't though. I was with the
naturist.'

'Bad luck. What did he do?'

'Nothing. He was a poet. He gave me his book of poems . . .'

Midnight and Bakersfield. Anne's blouse is definitely more
unbuttoned than previously. Without difficulty I can see the
whole of one small breast now, like a little poker-faced gentleman waiting behind a curtain before doing something wicked.

'Let's Eat Ranch BAKERSFIELD Motel' – the word 'Bakersfield' dropped into a slot for when the motel moves on. We
follow the red arrow to Cocktails, where we accept weak coffee,
weak hamburgers from a tired woman who lays overweight
arms on top of the till to rest them. Indians draped with
souvenirs approach this latest crop of passengers, but now we
must try to concentrate on the numbers and names coming over
the PA system like the odds in some game of chance in which we
are the runners. We are soon packed tight again in our familiar-

looking nests of jackets and scarves and biscuits in the newly laundered air, to be carried away into the night with our companions in chance huddled next to us. Spotlights falling on hands. Blonde hair hanging down.

6

SAN FRANCISCO

A Real Nice Routine

'Dear H,' said the message from my San Francisco contact, 'I am very much in India now, entirely and utterly fulfilling conscious/unconscious Promise of YUM. Blessings on your Poetry Journey. That can be very beautiful and penetrating Sadhana. Have you written your Greyhound poem yet? Do not worry about your reading. Bodhisattva will take care of everything.'

At first I thought this was an appeal to a god, but Bodhisattva turned out to be an actual person, very practical, who put me in touch with the right man at Berkeley and fixed me up with a deserted mattress in an un-made-up apartment on a hill, where I could hear the chains of the cable-cars whispering in their grooves at night. 'The hills are why it never snows in San Francisco,' he said, by way of recommending this chilly studio.

When he had gone, the first thing I did was scrap my 'Greyhound poem'.

Thom Gunn was out of town when I called, so I spent the first few days in cafés or shopping for records in The Wherehouse: sixties soul deletions for 50c. I went to the Vesuvio, the Corn Dog and the Sunlight Soda Fountain. I spent time in the Goodwill Store looking for cheap clothes to take home. If you wait long enough they announce 'Everything half price for the next half hour.' I was trying on a jacket once when an elderly black man came up and asked me if I was a female impersonator.

'No, I'm not, ' I said.

'I *seen* you,' said the man. 'You have the routine with the hat 'n stick. That's a real nice routine.'

He wanted to take me out and buy me 'a coupla drinks', but I said I had to buy all these things before the half hour was up.

'That your new costume?' he wanted to know. 'Can't you afford no customised piece by now?'

Another time I was shopping for boots on Mission Street. I wanted a pair of cheap flashy cowboy ones, but the cowboy assistant refused to admit that they didn't have any. He kept producing his classy tan 'reductions' and saying I was 'mighty cheeky' not to appreciate them.

'I'm making you some righteous proposals here,' he said, blocking my way to the door. 'Jus who the hell you think you are comin in here wastin ma time like that?'

Bodhisattva told me afterwards that he was a male prostitute and that the boots were just a cover, a way of discussing things. I'd probably insulted him deeply by insisting on something 'cheap and flashy' when he himself was so obviously young and wholesome. Plaid shirts were gay cruising gear, as were key-rings worn on the belt and/or bandanas hanging out of a back pocket, sado on the left (I think, but check on this), maso on the right.

After a few days I had the impression that everyone in San Francisco was homosexual and that those who weren't were definitely 'individualists' who didn't mind letting you know the fact to your face, usually in the street. 'You wanna fuck?' a middle-aged clerk asked me good-naturedly as I was waiting for a tram one morning. I looked at my watch and said 'five past twelve' before I realised what he'd said. I imagine he had an amusing story for the boys in the club that evening. 'You know that little drag queen, the one with the hat and stick . . . ?'

Well Son, What Kind of Stuff Do You Like?

'I have this weird sense of *time*,' a man at the next table in the Trieste Café was telling his friends. 'I can't believe North Beach is still here . . .'

'They should make it a Chinese-Italian enclave,' said someone else.

'I ever tell you guys about the time I was a fighter pilot in World War Two . . . ?'

'You know I think people are freaked out by the mere fact they survived . . .'

'In New York they don't think they're going to be wiped out. Why not for heaven's sake?'

'Sometimes I think we have been. In fact, if you want to talk mystically, there was a point when it happened. Round about 1968 it was . . .'

'Yeah. I met the enemy and he is us.'

At this point an old black man came into the café and starting handing round printed cards with plastic flowers attached to them 'PARDON ME. I am a DEAF MUTE. I am selling this CARD for a LIVING. PAY what you wish. THANK YOU and MAY GOD BLESS YOU.' He made a bomb.

'I have a secret to tell,' said one of the men. 'I bought eighty acres in Organ . . .'

'I got a farm in Texas . . .'

People in San Francisco are convinced they're going to slip down the Great Fault which runs through the city and through their lives. (Or else they think that driving on the right causes tornadoes.) Experts have come to the conclusion that the only thing left to do is to pour oil into the fault so the two sides can rub more smoothly. I wonder what God makes of that.

There is a sandwich man on Market Street who thinks everything will be all right if everyone drinks their own urine. Another advocates suicide. The majority settle for a kind of galloping sentimentality which reminds me of London. In Progressive Nostalgia the albino proprietor, eyes slithering back and forth, put his peculiar arm round my shoulder and said, 'Well, son, what kind of stuff do *you* like?' – as if it was the most natural thing in the world to have an obsession with old prophylactic packs, fifties sorority buttons, hub-caps and 78 rpm gramophone needle boxes. 'Oh, I like it all,' I said, buying a non-committal Brigitte Bardot postcard and edging back into the daylight where he could not follow.

Out in the street a New Orleans jazz band was playing 'St Louis Blues'.

When I got through to Thom Gunn he said there was a memorial concert by Jefferson Airplane in Ashbury Park that afternoon. He'd see me there. I remembered his epigram to that group in *Moly*: 'The music comes and goes on the wind/comes and goes on the brain.' I never liked the folksy, limp-wristed sound of the Bay Area groups, but this was a rare re-run. I made it out to the park, scene of the original love-ins, in a spirit of anthropological enquiry and I wasn't disappointed. The misty, muddy valley was full to the brim with excited hippies in pixie caps and wall-hangings, miming the ecstasies of their youth while their grave, undernourished children looked on. Their distinctive forward-leaning lope brought back visits to London's Arts Lab years ago. A small contingent of the Hell's Angels had turned out for the occasion and were doing their best to bring the statutory bad vibe to bear on one corner of the crowd.

'Fuckin' Angels, man!'

'Fuckin' Altamont!'

A Red Cross ambulance was already filling up with panicking trippers.

At the far end of the valley, as if disappearing finally through the wrong end of time's telescope, Jefferson Airplane played or didn't play to rapturous acceptance. Of Thom Gunn there was no sign. Messages were being put over the PA at one point, so I struggled forward and handed in my scrap of paper.

'Thom Gunn is waiting for Hugo outside the First Aid tent,' came the message.

'Are you Thom Gunn?' asked a kindly girl.

'No, I'm looking for him,' I said.

'Thom Gunn?' said someone else. 'He was talking to Mustapha. He had these kittens . . .'

Mustapha was sitting in the middle of the crowd playing the lute. He had seen Thom, naturally. They had all seen him, but . . . Why didn't I ask Bones? He had given Bones one of his kittens . . .

Bones, when I found her, was tripping heavily and in no state to foster a cloakroom ticket, let alone a kitten. She looked like a crazy version of Mrs Charles Addams and had already performed some sinister magic on the animal.

'What kitten?' she asked, rolling blacked-in eyes.

'Never mind about the kitten,' I said. 'Have you seen Thom?'

'Thom who?'

'Thom Gunn.'

'Thom Gunn!' said Bones, gripping my arm in her claw. 'What kind of heavy name is that, man?'

'I don't know,' I said.

Bones rolled her eyes and went galloping off into the crowd.

'You wanna toke on this?' said the girl I had first spoken to.

'Thanks.'

I had a toke on this and was soon wondering why I was feeling like a dead oak tree.

'What is it?' I stammered.

'Angel dust,' said the girl, whose name seemed to be Why-me? 'You wannanothertoke?'

'What's angel dust?' I said.

'Dunno. Embalming fluid isn't it, Jake?'

'Pig tranquilliser,' moaned Jake.

'I thought it was nuclear waste,' said another girl, who wasn't smoking.

We Operate as a Charity Here. We Sell Indulgences If You Like

The Haight area of San Francisco resembles Notting Hill Gate – the hills, the stucco, the homeliness, music with the bass turned up coming under psychedelic blinds, the same slightly dated lives being clung to, grown men roller-skating to the shops, others strolling arm in arm, flinging challenging glances. I think Why-Me?'s friends were showbusiness drop-outs of some kind, living in what looked like the lap of luxury on angel dust, food stamps and old Grateful Dead posters. One of them was a conjuror. His new wife – or was it his 'new-wife'? – sang to an instrument of sea-shells and fuse-wire: a whistling, bat-like delivery which made me draw back in horror. Though living as man and wife and having a baby zonked on angel dust fumes, these two both declared themselves to be 'gay'.

'Did you know over half the population of San Francisco is gay?' asked Why-Me? happily.

'Two-thirds,' said the conjuror.

'You have your own department stores and everything, I believe,' I said uneasily.

'You gay?' snapped the conjuror, looking me in the eye.
'No,' I said, blushing badly.
'You don't find too many chicks giving head in your country is that right?' stated the conjuror.
'Oh I don't know,' I said. 'They will if you ask them nicely.'
'If you ask them nicely. Is that so?'
'Of course that's right, Zeno,' said his new-wife sweetly. 'The practice originates over here so you don't expect . . .'
'I had an insight into that one time,' said Why-Me?, her thoughts trailing off into angel dust.
'Are you really a conjuror?' I asked.
'Zeno's a psychic conjuror,' said his new-wife. 'He transforms people's lives.'
'What into?' I asked.
'Smoke,' said Zeno disarmingly. 'No, seriously. We operate as a charity here. We sell indulgences if you like.'
'How do you mean?'
'A person comes to us with a meditation problem, we create an exclusive mantra for that person, advise him how to use it and so on.'
The man was a guru! What he was describing to me was a business where one person sells a word to someone else. Not bad. When I asked (for my own interest) whether it could be just any word, like 'smithereens' or 'Jacksonville', Zeno said no, it couldn't, and wouldn't say another word unless I wanted to buy one myself. I discovered later that he had sold Why-Me? 'Alhambra', which seemed a bit facile, but Why-Me? said it had got her through her exams and was well worth the $10, so why not? Then we had some more angel dust on the roof and Why-Me? asked me if I would like to go back to her place to see her father's barbed wire collection. Was her father there too? Sure, said Why-Me? reassuringly.

You Can't Leave Now, I Might Die

'Er . . . this is Thom Gunn,' said Why-Me?, introducing me to her father's darkened bedroom. 'Oh no, I'm sorry, it isn't Thom Gunn, is it, but this is Daddy, anyway . . .' Her father wore a jellaba and a ponytail and was evidently tripping, as were we.
'Any calls, Daddy?'
'Your Mom called. She didn't speak, of course.'

'This is my room,' said Why-Me?, showing me into a beautiful first-floor apartment overlooking the Golden Gate. 'You want some blackcurrant cordial?'

'No thanks.'

We sat looking at the sunset for a while, then, for something to do, we rolled up the last of the angel dust and began turning into wall hangings again. This was the most inhuman effect I have ever experienced. I quite enjoyed going completely autistic, but Why-Me? wasn't so sure. She asked me about nine times, very politely, whether I would care for some blackcurrant cordial, then she burst into tears and said she wanted her Mommy.

'Mommy-Mommy,' she called up the stairs.

'Yes, hon,' said her Dad.

'I want Mommy,' said Why-Me? 'Where's my Mommy?'

'Mom's in Brooklyn, hon. You know that.'

'I want my Mommy.' She picked up the phone and started to dial numbers, occasionally bashing the rest with the side of her other hand and shrieking into the void. After a while she got the operator.

'Operator? I gotta find my Mom,' she moaned, 'I'm freaking out in here. You gotta help me. Yeah. Brooklyn. Yeah. New York. I don't know. Bardoman Asteritch, I think. Mom? Mom? Oh. OK, I'll wait. Mom? Is that you? Listen, I wanna talk to Mrs Belasco. No, Mrs Belasco. What? Oh my Gard . . .'

Why-Me? finally got through to someone in Europe, who gave her a fearful row and made her weep and weep even more, curled up like a baby and sucking her thumb, or opening her eyes very wide for a moment's reality and asking me sweetly if I'd like another glass of blackcurrant cordial, which, finally, I accepted. As she poured the glutinous fluid she caught sight of the bruise from the telephone struggle beginning to show on her hand.

'Look at that,' she screamed, forgetting the drink completely. 'The blood's all caught up. I can't feel my hand. It's going gangrenous. My Gard!'

I looked at the hand and sure enough it seemed to my doctored imagination that it was indeed gangrenous. There was even a funny smell in the air. I didn't want her shrieking any more, so I kept quiet about it. We soon had other things to worry about.

'I think my pulse is skipping,' said Why-Me? 'I don't feel so good.'

She opened her shirt and tried to get me to listen to her heart. I put my ear to her breast and had to admit that I couldn't hear anything except her father's Grateful Dead record coming from downstairs. Why-Me? did some deep breathing, then she got into bed and went to sleep. I began to creep from the room.

'Where you going?'

'Home.'

'You can't leave me now. I might die. My father's always trying to get into my pants. Come here.' She began undoing my trousers. 'Get into bed,' she said.

Life in the Middle Ages

When I got into bed, Why-Me? asked me if I wanted some blackcurrant. I said no and she told me her heart had stopped again, staring at me through the semi-darkness with panic-stricken eyes. I tried to calm her down, but it was no good. This time she had decided she was too fat. That was why I couldn't hear her heart. And wasn't fatness the main cause of heart disease? She got hold of pieces of her fairly taut flesh and showed them to me in disgust.

'Look, look, it's all fat,' she said. 'Can't you massage me? I want to get rid of it, get rid of it. Boo hoo hoo.'

Why-Me?'s face was spotty, but her body was strong and smooth and her large legs had a convulsive, lobster-like existence. I had to rub and pummel her all over for about half an hour, while she cried for her Mom and told me over and over again how fat she was. Eventually, when she was once more restored to thinness, she said she would do the same for me if I liked. I said it was all right, but she wouldn't listen. From the way she pushed me around, got me up against the wall, then pushed my head under the bedclothes as if I was her teddy bear, it was hard to believe this girl was having a nervous breakdown.

Finally she seemed satisfied and whimpered herself to sleep on top of me so I couldn't run away. Sex with Why-Me? was like life in the Middle Ages: nasty, brutish and short. It was an evening when, as she informed me next morning, 'Nothing Happened Between Us.'

Slowly I recovered. I don't remember how I got home. I lay on my mattress and fought off crazy conjurors and crowds of hippy kittens. Cable cars dragged me up and down hills. I had to find Thom Gunn by Wednesday, but he too was in disguise . . .

One day I woke up and there was Andy from Iowa, come to escort me to the reading.

Andy was a huge Jewish schoolboy of about thirty, very nervous and shabby and ambitious, who said if I didn't object he would join me on the platform and read a few translations. I said I didn't object and Andy said anyway the entire African and Oriental Studies Dept would be turning out to get a sneak preview of his thesis on the Persian poet Hafiz, the Nightingale of Shiraz, so the Hall wouldn't be completely empty for once.

I was delighted to have this character reading with me as it meant I wouldn't have to read first. When he asked me if I would mind reading first I said I would mind, and I wouldn't toss him for it. I think it was this that started him on his fly-button checks.

At first it was hardly more noticeable than a quick straightening of the tie. But once he was up there on the stage, his flies on a level with the eyes of the entire African and Oriental Studies Dept, the tick matured rapidly and his hand was soon going to the top of his zipper about once every five seconds. I was fascinated by this and felt relaxed for once. Did he imagine his compulsion was masked by the book he was holding? Or did he think our minds were flying around twelfth-century Shiraz with the (untranslatable) Nightingale?

After a while I noticed he didn't touch his zip while he was actually speaking, but only in the pauses, like a kind of punctuation mark. He would say a line, glance at the ceiling, check his flies, say another line and so on. I tried to see if there was any rhythmical connection between line-breaks and fly-checks and sure enough you got a little flurry of checks at the beginning of a poem, then fewer and fewer as it got under way, ending with a massive hitch-check-hitch, as if someone was actually trying to de-bag him.

There was an expression of vast relief on his face when after about an hour he finally relinquished the platform and rejoined his friends from the Dept.

Adjusting my own clothing, I mounted the stage and read. Andy was in the front row, legs stretched out, at ease. Every time I looked up, a thing I force myself to do, even though it makes me dizzy, I caught sight of him checking the time on his watch.

'I've got to the point now,' a trembling professor was telling his students at the drinks afterwards, 'where I realise that I'm not well known therefore I must be good. It took me some time before I realised that.'

'I think you underestimate yourself, Jim,' one of his students told him. 'You're nothing like as unknown as you sometimes make out.'

A Letter from My Sweetheart

Thom had left for England the day before. He'd called while I was 'out'. There was nothing to keep me in San Francisco now, so I decided to move on to Los Angeles and April Stanley – Anne too if her father hadn't retrieved her yet. Perhaps the reading there would be more . . . fertile.

Before catching the night bus I took myself to dinner in Chinatown. I went to a restaurant where the portly Chinese owner said, 'How ya doin', Mac? All light? This very raid-back Chink nosh house. Y'all c'mon back now, y'hear? Light on!' and then the Coffee Gallery where Janis Joplin first sang. There was a black crooner there, a cross between Harry Belafonte and Donovan, singing 'Nature Boy' to two white nuns drinking capuccinos. Nobody asked me what I wanted so I said 'Goodnight, everyone' and left. Outside on the sidewalk a young orthodox Jew was playing English music hall songs on a ten-inch-high toy piano . . . Always plenty of 'crossover' in San Francisco.

On Fisherman's Wharf I put in 25c to get a 'Letter from My Sweetheart' (April?):

Sweet Angel Child [it said], yes, you are the dearest sweetest kindest purest boy I ever met, but once is enough! I don't want to adopt a boy to raise – I want a he-man, Sweetheart, one who smokes, drinks, swears an' everything. You are entirely too good for this earth as a man, but you might join the Women's League, learn to knit tidily or watch the babies as a nurse girl. No, I don't play 'tiddle-de-winks', 'drop the handkerchief' or 'London Bridge is Falling Down'. If you want to do something to please me just play 'You are a Little Bluebird' and fly away to stay.

Two or three days after I spent the night in Why-Me?'s untidy bunk I felt an itching in my pants and pulling them down was just in time to catch one of those irritating little beasts trying to make a dash for cover. Another, imagining itself to be invisible, had bedded down in the open. With some difficulty I prized it from my skin and flicked it out of the window. The way the size of these creatures relates to one's diminishing vision is perhaps nature's way of telling one to stay home in the evenings. I was just wondering what you do about crabs in America when I remembered Thom Gunn's poem, 'The first time I got crabs, I/experienced positively/Swiftian self-revulsion: me/unclean! But now I think instead/"I must get some A200." '
  'A tub or a tube, sir?'
  'A tube will do, thanks.'
  For the first time in my life a poem proved of practical use. I put on the A200 and everyone lived (or died) happily ever after.

7
LOS ANGELES & APRIL STANLEY

Hollywood Next Seven Exits

The words 'Passport to Enchantment' fold back out of sight as I enter the midnight bus for Los Angeles and find a window seat on the right.

The usual tortoise-women, western heroes and music hall acts haunt the central aisle in search of human weakness. (Plenty.) I leave my coat where it is on the seat. I see a mad lady with an Ophelia hair-wreath has got in the wrong queue, twitching all over with revoked decisions. A cake-walk-style black dandy asks me for change. He has on an elaborate green monkey suit and buff bowler, with which he bows. Oh God, he has the same transistor as me. I'm snapped. No no, I'm sure they're made in Japan. Is that all? A bit of zydeco! He says he likes Joni Mitchell and America. Oh I see, the group! Now isn't that typical? Yes, it is my coat I'm afraid. Shall I put it up? He sits down, saying he won't be disturbing me as he has to learn his lines for *The Life of Captain Cook*. I say this is interesting and he tells me he is an acrobat and a comedian and has been on the US Space Programme. Yes, the real one, at Kennedy! He takes out a handkerchief and pulls it through his fist suggestively. From the way he smiles I know it has changed colour, but the sodium street lighting makes the green and red look the same. Before long I am hearing him his lines, which are in pidgin.

Oakland – the sleeping station looks like the inside of a

fridge, candle-drip interns pushing trolleys marked with the names of cities. Two force-fed double-women pucker their lips disgustedly to kiss one another goodbye. The bus lurches to one side for a moment, then oozes out into the night.

Chunky hills scattered with scrub loom through the dawn. Nicer ones are sprinkled with bungalows. A neon JESUS IS COMING goes on and off as if changing its mind. HOLLYWOOD NEXT SEVEN EXITS.

The Educated Car Wash has young girls in mini-skirts and mortar-boards. Royal palms hang dead branches in North Hollywood. 'Lodge B. Gay (Vacancy)'. THE MOVIELAND/MOTEL HAS CLOSED/CIRCUIT TELEVISION/'Join the Marina Del Ray: Community For Relaxed Living. Heated Pool. Singles Apartments.' We pass a store where they hire giant papier-mâché heads of film stars, cypress trees and prehistoric animals. An alighting pterodactyl guards the severed head of Charlie Chaplin. A butch cop with a gun guards the Youngtown Senior Citizen Community. 'The Western Exterminator Company Is Under N w Man gem nt.'

'Sometimes I just can't believe I'm not famous,' says the black man sympathetically.

'I know exactly what you mean.'

'You know what I think? I think this is gonna be ma lucky dee!'

Sunset Boulevard. Heart beating now. The rush-hour jam on Hoover Street . . .

A Poor Boy on the Line

I was discovering that downtown Los Angeles isn't where you have to be in Los Angeles. It's where you arrive, or end up. All the fun has moved west, as usual. Everyone in my address book lived in the western suburbs, but I couldn't reach any of them, even the ones I knew. It wasn't long before I was having an attack of lizard-itis, seated on my too-heavy suitcases opposite a fortuneteller's which said 'YOUR FUTURE IS HERE'. Have some breakfast, I thought, and you'll feel better. Then a passer-by stuck his finger in my eye showing another passer-by the way back to the Greyhound Bus Station.

April Stanley was the prettiest girl I knew in America and she lived right there in Los Angeles. The idea that at any given moment every single person has to be somewhere in the world is either worrying or comforting, depending on your mood. The trouble with April was that she seemed to have risen in the world since I met her as a courier in Paris a few years ago.

'April can't talk right now as her boss is talking,' explained her secretary.

'What is her boss boss of?'

'Why, MGM,' said the secretary in surprise.

'Hold on a sec.'

From where I was I could see a policeman about to walk off with my suitcases.

'What you got in here?' he said.

'Records mostly.'

'Open up, I'll have to check on that.'

I have a hard-to-support habit of buying old rhythm and blues albums whenever I'm depressed. By now I had about eighty-six and I could hardly lift them and wanted another one urgently.

'Little Anthony and the Imperials!' said the cop incredulously. 'You like that stuff?'

'Quite,' I said. 'You know . . . What kind of stuff do *you* like?'

'Joni Mitchell, The Eagles, Village People. We got the hi-fi in the interrogation room.'

'Right. That's the real thing. Neil Diamond.'

'Right. OK. You can move on now.'

I told April's secretary that I would call back in the morning, then I dragged my cases to the nearest drugstore and had a coffee and started to feel worse again.

Back Projection on Wilshire Boulevard

I was staring into my address book, as into a deep well, when I suddenly remembered Anne, the Jewish girl on the bus from Bakersfield. An office gave me a number in Santa Barbara and a man was soon telling me to come on over, Anne was in the shower. Her new name was 'Amy Loving'.

With Amy's dripping body dancing before my eyes, I checked both suitcases and boarded the next bus. (Luggage is an unnecessary warning to a prospective host.)

We had been travelling for about half an hour down the same endless road when I started to think I must have missed my stop. I asked the driver and he said, 'Look at your watch in half an hour,' so I sat back and tried to enjoy the scenery. Bank, temple, gas station, motel, bank, temple, gas station, the endless forecourts of Wilshire Boulevard seemed to be on a loop, like some half-hearted attempt at back projection. Everything was slightly out of focus, like early colour film. I looked around inside the bus and noticed it had been slowly filling up with the very old. Clinging to handles like victims of a holocaust, these senior citizens looked as if they had come straight from the funeral parlour. Yet they had a lonely determination about them. Too old to drive, too full of vitamins to stay home, they were giving the driver hell, as if these were still the good old days and he was their Filipino chauffeur. Were they the last inhabitants of this vast, exhausted suburb?

'Stop here, driver. My Henry should be along . . . I can't see him yet.'

'Driver, I want the third Crocker on Wilshire. Will you let me know?'

'Make a right here, driver. It isn't far . . .' (Americans don't bother *turning* right, it's more American to *make* one.)

I was amazed to see the long-suffering individual going along with all their suggestions, just as if we were all in a musical together.

Despite detours, we were now at McArthur Park, where Richard Harris left his cake out in the non-existent Southern California rain. I watched the old folks peering out of their windows at the life-size models of dinosaurs and brontosauri standing about in the scrub and it seemed to me that these melancholy giants looked back at them with a certain sympathy.

Someone Very Big Indeed Playing God

The apartment was a gay film-world crash-pad belonging to a New York image-therapist called Duke Heinz, now absent. It had fallen into the hands of student Hans Haltmann, who opened the door in his robe and launched straight into the plot of his 'new' movie. It was difficult to explain, he explained, though basically it was a story of prejudice and liberation in a Third World country, which he named as Australia. Did I know that aboriginals could stand on one leg for a week? Had I ever seen a genuine Samurai sword such as this one? Hans had a Cadillac, he told me, and he kept fit with the aid of Japanese sword practice and (a wink) bisexuality. What was I into?

I watched Hans posing with his sword for a while, then Amy came back from the shops, seemed to recognise me from someplace and started telling me about her new life in 'motion pictures', which was going to teach her father a lesson he'd never forget. She had a contract, she said, with Hans's 'parent company' and was going to make a religio-space-creepy called *The Second Coming*, with someone very big indeed playing God, she couldn't say who. Amy had dyed her hair white and she wore a tight white skirt, white sunglasses (up) and white shoes with red Louis XIV heels, a great improvement on the demure virgin I had cuddled in the Greyhound. But did she remember me? I said casually that I was looking for a place to stay and she introduced me to two shadowy 'members of the team' who were lingering strangely in a large bare room hung with boomerangs: Solly and Hidenao. There were other rooms, but I couldn't see into them. When she showed me her own room I noticed that it was already equipped with a heavy-set, crew-cut Adonis whom Amy referred to as Style.

'You Australian?' said Style easily.

'No.'

'New Zealand?'

'No.'

'Looking for a lawyer?'

'No.'

'I know one can get you a green card in three weeks and no hassle.'

'I might take you up on that.'

Amy winked at me to secure my indulgence.

'He's always trying to help people out, aren't you, Style?' she said, putting her hand into his shirt. 'Style can lift me up in one hand and hold me above his head, can't you, Style?'

Later I took them both to dinner in an expensive sauna complex with yodelling and kebabs and spent the night alone in a hotel.

Walking on the Moon

I rang April next day, but she was still casting and so was her boss. I felt sure her secretary was pronouncing my name wrong.

It sounded like 'sugar' when she repeated it back to me on the phone. I decided to go in to the studio myself, fell asleep on the bus and had to walk back down Hollywood Boulevard in a kind of sand-storm, seeing only the names of the stars set in the sidewalk inside big Stars of David: George Allen, Roy Rogers, Marilyn Monroe. The only new ones are Armstrong, Aldrin and Collins and Liza Minnelli. You walk along, then you notice the list repeating itself: George Allen, Roy Rogers . . . They even have Rin Tin Tin.

'No, I'm afraid Miss Stanley is on location.'

'May I leave a note?'

'By all means.'

'Thank you.'

'Have a nice day!'

A minute later I was back in the street, searching my photo of April for a clue to my fate. A Range Rover cruised by and a bunch of girls yelled out 'What's happening?'

'Nothing!' I yelled back.

That's no good in the States. It's like saying 'I don't speak English' or 'I'm sick'. You have to pick up your cards or they deal you out next time. As Amy reminded me, 'We have more things to do in this country than any other country in the world.'

The Land of the Kiss

But it's difficult getting started. All around you beautiful women pose with their mouths open and their legs up, yet when you have bought their airline-promises, their cigarette-metaphors, there they are, dripping with it all still.

'Now here's a flavour that doesn't quit on ya,' they chew, '' 'n I lahk that.'

'My near-naked body is the equivalent of an erection,' they seem to be sneering, 'so what're you gonna do about it?'

Walking the streets, there is this underlying sensation of impotence in the air, as it is borne in on you that you cannot answer their challenge. You buy your way out of it as often as you can, but the hoardings follow you home. When you get there the tv is waiting behind the door, the magazines open in the bathroom, the newspapers on the kitchen floor. You look out of the window and a wonder-woman air-sock is dragging the words 'I'M BUTTERKIST' through sperm-flecked clouds. A Kentucky chicklet knocks on your fried door. You hand over everything you have, but you know she will be there again tomorrow. Then you get on the phone to your mother.

There Is a Fog upon LA

Desperate measures are called for. I decide to have the photo of April and me blown up to poster size. I'm going to leave it, signed, at the desk for her.

I take the picture to the studio, but when I get inside they think I am trying to trick my way into acting, this being the casting side. They tell me to go round the back, to the trades-men's entrance, in order to be processed.

'Can't you see?' I say. 'It's a picture of April and me . . .'

'April . . . ?'

'April Stanley.'

'April Stanley. Oh yes. You can leave it here if you like, OK? We'll let you know, all right? Have a nice day.'

Have an epileptic fit, but be sure and have a REALLY nice day. That's the main thing.

The Furthest-Out Black Studies Programme on the Coast

'So! You're a poet!' said Hans when we met next evening at Alice's Restaurant. 'I tell you we may be getting Steve Stills for Resident Singer-Songwriter next semester? This is Jocko, by the way, my cameraman. Jocko used to play bass with The Sleeve.'

Hans was involved with poetry himself, he said, especially committed poetry, and thought it could be very visual if handled properly. We had something expensive to eat, then Hans led me up the hill to the University, where I was due to read. He was a medical student, he told me, although he was really into 'Neechy, Anarchy and Hessy'.

'The University has a radical approach to politics,' he said, buying us ice-creams in the Orangerie, 'otherwise we could never survive here. For instance, we have one of the furthest-out Black Studies Programmes on the Coast, and I guess that means the world.'

As we walked through the College gardens the sound of steel guitars came to us on hibiscus-scented air. Everywhere bands were rehearsing, groups convening, parties limbering up. We skirted what Hans said was the largest training hospital in the world and came to a theatre where a number of actors were rehearsing. The play, a black nativity, was to form the opening sequence to his own film, *Rights of Passage*. The birth of a black baby into the hostile atmosphere of an all-white delivery ward was to be inter-cut with scenes from Louis XIV's Versailles. Hans had borrowed lights, drips, uniforms and beds from the training hospital.

'Don't you see?' he said. 'It's the perfect metaphor. Hygiene. Consumer paranoia. Catch-22. These things . . .' he indicated a tray of clamps and breaches, 'they're an obstruction, not an aid to birth. They encourage . . . you know . . . Caesarean . . . and I don't have to tell you what *that* means in terms of *Society* . . .'

'No.'

We watched the play for a while, then I asked Hans to show me the way to the Hendrix Room, where I was already overdue. Hans wasn't too keen to quit the rehearsal right now, he said. It was important for him to be there. Would I mind if he found his own way to the reading later on? Then it was a matter of running fast down every corridor I could find until I came to a poster billing me as 'The Editor of the *New Review*' and popping up like the White Rabbit in a brilliantly lit crowded lecture hall.

Half way through the reading, the door opened and lights and cameras burst into the place, as if a game of blind man's buff had overflowed from a party somewhere. Hans was holding Jocko from behind and directing him towards the platform where I was reading a poem about Aborigines. A sound man crouched and ran from place to place like a storm trooper.

At the end, Hans put up his hand for a question. Camera and sound zoomed in his direction. He liked the poem about my daughter, he said, but did 'Martinique great-grandmother' mean she was black? The camera swung round to me and I said it didn't. Hans looked disappointed by this. He wanted to know whether I had attended the birth, and what I felt about it. For instance, had my wife been obliged to lie on her back, like a dead person? If so, had I protested? I said she had, but that she hadn't minded, so I hadn't. I felt there was another position Hans wanted to promote, but I wasn't going to let him. I took another question concerning the poetry of Leonard Cohen. Did I ever sing my work, the professor wanted to know. If not, why not?

'I really liked the reading by the way,' said Hans later. 'I was hoping you'd join us on the set tomorrow. See what you think of the Aborigine scene . . .'

What Do You Think of It So Far?

When I got there a distressed white woman in a surgical mask and strait-jacket was being moved into position on a hospital bed, her feet in stirrups. Filming commenced and a wet black doll duly made its appearance, upside down, in the hairy fist of a white doctor who I thought for a second was going to bite it.

'Cut,' said Hans.

A change of drapes and we were in Versailles, where one of Louis's mistresses was about to give birth. It was Louis, Hans informed me, who started the 'disgusting' fashion for women to give birth lying on their backs. He liked to watch, apparently, and he couldn't see enough when they used the squatting birth-stool. 'That abomination,' he called it.

From Hans's tone I gathered that he didn't share Louis's taste. With his over-anxious imagination and whatever scraps came to hand he had fashioned a mock-up of a birth-stool, which he now wheeled on. From a distance it looked like the top of a waste-shoot put together from pieces of ironbark, its elaborate padded wing-pieces decorated with fruit labels. The contraption was even furnished with a head-rest, taken from a Continental car, presumably to take care of any recoil occasioned by the birth. It even had a rudimentary reading stand, for the quieter moments, with a leatherbound book on it and the book-mark hanging down. No effort had been spared.

From the moment Hans proudly unveiled his creation, everyone knew that it was the star. No matter what anyone else said or did, the eye was drawn irresistibly back to it. Was it a rickshaw or a rubber dinghy? A hip-bath or a sedan chair? One person said it looked to him like an old orgone accumulator. Someone else thought it had once been part of a wind tunnel. The only thing one could say with any certainty was that it had a French look to it. And that it had lots of star quality.

Grotesquely upstaged by this impregnable abstraction, the white woman was now required to give birth in it again. She looked like a frightened child astride a runaway Golden Galloper.

'Roll!' said Hans with satisfaction.

It was now that Louis XIV stormed on to the set.

'Not like that. Not like that, you fools,' he cried. 'We've told you before. We can't see if it's ours that way. It might be a blackamoor for all we know.'

'Cut,' said Hans. 'We need someone to hold the banner while Bo is gesticulating.'

'I'll hold it,' I said.

'Could you make like you were shouting something,' said Hans. 'But don't say anything, right?'

'Sure,' I said, commencing to mouth.

'Don't move your mouth so much,' said Hans, already irritated. 'Look, can you come back tomorrow?'

'I don't think I can,' I apologised.

'Christ! Style, for Chrissake fix the end of the banner to that gum tree or something.'

The courtiers now picked up the unwilling woman and laid her out on a table set for dinner, Louis drew his sword and in due course the wet black doll made another appearance: close-up of Louis's blacked-up face registering horror.

'Cut,' yelled Hans in triumph. 'Take five everyone.'

Outside, in the cool grounds of UCLA, a nubile student was doing a form of hula dance for friends who sucked on ice-creams. A variety of well-established gum trees shaded the lovers lying on the grassy slopes overlooking prim Westwood. Joints could be seen going round and a luminous frisbee (a 'Moonlighter') hung in the air for a moment, like a giant firefly, before completing its leisurely arc.

'What do you think of it so far?' said Hans.

The word 'rubbish' sprang naturally to my lips.

'Incredible,' I said, remembering the large, empty apartment. 'Fantastic.'

'You really think so?'

'Yes I do.'

'Listen, where you staying while you're in LA?'

April's Fool

At the hotel there was a message from April leaving her new home number. I had to ring three times in order to get all kinds of loving messages on to her answerphone, which had Marlene

Dietrich singing 'I'm the Laziest Girl in Town'. When I'd done it I wished I hadn't, but you can't wipe it out, so I rang back claiming to have been drunk (bad): couldn't wipe that out either.

April rang back (good), inviting me to dinner (good) with her English (bad) live-in (bad) boyfriend (bad), whom someone had told me was bi (bad or good?). This was a visit to the Empire State Building of my imagination, but now the lift had come I didn't want to go up.

April was all I remembered, however: clean-limbed, ahead-of-fashion, laughing secretly over her beautiful shoulder to me as she fixed my drink, the high-tech brush-work on her cheekbones making a fetish of perfection, camera-angles flashing.

'Your face was invented by a master,' I stammered idiotically as we pored over the photograph I had sent to her office. It was an ordinary street-snap, which I'd picked up after she'd left Paris for good. I'd had the original in my wallet for years and the jumbo blow-up showed clearly the ageing fold-marks running down between us. April said she thought of it as coming from the distant past when she was still young. What was I doing now though?

'Me? Oh, you know . . . actually . . .'

Actually, what *was* I doing?

The answer was that I was doing the same thing I'd been doing in Paris: hanging around cafés picking up poems, in the hope of writing beautiful girls. Nothing, in fact.

'I'm working on a film script,' I said.

'Oh really? Who for?'

'Haltmann.'

'Who?'

'Haltmann. Hans Haltmann. I think he's very . . . you know . . . young . . .'

April's smile — a sort of thermostat of how one was doing — reminded me that interesting news was not what you thought, but who you knew and where you'd been. Hadn't I been at school with Prince William or someone? April had been poor I remembered (those were the days) and her smile had always frowned on anything Low Rent. Poetry produced this effect in her, as did the word 'Greyhound'.

'Barney, what are you doing out there,' she called. 'Come here . . . What's happened to Marie-Georges?'

Barney, April's 'interface', came in carrying vegetarian cheese and crackers. April had told me that he was an actor, 'a good one, a natural in fact,' but you could see straight away that he was her hobby, her little weakness, her Continental car. A handsome, camp remittance man, Barney's only serious problem in life was what next to put on April's stereo.

'Listen to this, listen to this,' he thrilled, turning up Osibisa. 'The bass, the bass line . . . oop oop pe-doop . . . poo poo pe-doo . . .'

'Isn't he a *nut*?' said April when Barney danced back into the kitchen. 'You wouldn't think he had a serious side, would you?'

Marie-Georges, an attractive French actress whom April was agenting for, wasn't in the same light-as-air mood as her hosts. She was in pain from a poisoned foot and she looked tense and tired in her black shift.

'Ain't the US of A-mazing?' grinned Barney. But Marie-Georges didn't check on this. Her doctor was milking her and she needed a green card urgently. When Barney praised America's achievements in Art, Space and Athletics she said she thought the United States was too big a proportion of the globe to be admirable in itself.

'What about Hollywood?' said the Hon. Barney, 'And rock 'n roll?'

'Extensions of Europe,' said Marie-Georges.

'The film I'm making at the moment is about early Hollywood, and believe me . . .'

Here Marie-Georges, who had never been in a film, was obliged to yield to Barney, who we were supposed to know had been sodomised in a recent Italian epic. The trouble was he wouldn't stop telling us about it. Unless, of course, we had something to say about it ourselves, in which case he deferred to us, fondly offering us a 'ciggy'. If we asked him a direct question about the film, like we were supposed to, he stood up, clapped hands, ran out of the room, reappeared in a funny hat, did a little dance, then ran around on top of the furniture shrieking like a gibbon and spilling everyone's drink. If you were lucky you didn't get a kiss at the end of it. This was cute, April thought.

'Honourable, you're too much,' she said, blind with love.

Dinner came and went, an elaborate piece of theatre created by Barney 'for April and her guests'. Everyone applauded. All I

could think of to do was to light a stream of cigarettes, as if
making a little flame could restore one's charisma, or having
smoke in one's lungs make everything all right in the world. I
had no energy, no dope, and I broke their record-player trying
to put on Brenda Lee.

'Oh No!' went Barney. 'Now we can't play Cole Porter's
poetry. Did you know he was gay and wrote all this gay poetry?
April tells me you're a poet yourself, Hugh . . .'

'Well . . .'

'Do you mind my asking something?'

'No, what?'

'Are you gay by any chance?'

'No, are you?'

'Let's say I have been known to suck cock,' said the Hon.
Barney, closing long-lashed eyes.

'Honourable, you're OUTRAGEOUS!' said April Stanley
lovingly.

I tried not to cry.

Show me a man who laughs at defeat and I'll show you a
happy chiropodist.

The End of the Western World

Terrifying old vultures and walruses in immaculate linen and
panamas populate these lively buses linking Los Angeles. Their
horny hands cling to seat-backs for dear life. Their dimmed
eyes hope for landmarks. Outcasts of families, they're going to
manage this thing if it kills them and it makes them mad. What
must it be like, after a lifetime of trying, to end up an inaccurate
model of yourself? One blue-eyed waxwork from the silent
era – white rings in her eyes big as hula hoops – makes a grab
past me to haul herself towards her grave. Her weathered skull
can barely hold on to its bits of haunted hair. She whispers, 'It's
hell to be old. Hell! I had a chauffeured Packard when I was
your age. Not any more. Oh No!' She looks a hundred. And the
blind too abound, their shoes polished, their bow-ties neat, the
tips of their canes dipped in red for some reason. These strange
vehicles are like parties in Valhalla with the long-suffering
driver as MC.

So many octogenarians are asking where we are I feel
ashamed to, but there's no chance of overshooting this time.

Santa Monica is THE END OF THE WESTERN WORLD. The freeway goes straight on to the pier and the pier sticks out into the Pacific and that's it. There's a road on the pier and wonderful old fifties cars cruise up and down it, massive rounded body-work almost touching the ground all round. Cars as well as people last longer on the Coast as they don't rust so fast.

There is fairground music coming from the pier, so I walk along it and come to an ancient merry-go-round house. This must be where *The Sting* was filmed. I remember April telling me that when she was growing up in Los Angeles she used to think that everywhere in the world had a film being made in it.

A Message from the Horses

Our thanks to the citizens of Santa Monica who voted to save our pier. The house where we live is the only apartment house in the world to have a merry-go-round and an organ (built in Germany in 1900). Many famous people come to visit this building, including your parents and grandparents, so follow in their footsteps, come aboard, close your eyes and forget your troubles. My brothers and sisters have been on the pier 80 years. We have no place to go. This is our home and we want to die here. Sincerely yours, the 49 horses on the merry-go-round.

Bright red flowering trees called bottle-brushes express my happiness to be wandering around this seedy grandiose suburb where people still walk a little. The peeling Regency blocks on the front, the pier, the vine-laden palisades, remind me of Brighton. Here at last is the acceptable face of Los Angeles! Cross the Corniche by a footbridge, step over a miniature railroad, thread between bulging beach huts where whole families seem to be living, on to the pebbly beach – smell of tar and fish and salt. On the prom under the pier are all manner of ordinary and extraordinary folk having fun: students and blacks and chicanos: the old, the halt and the strange. A rubbery black boy bounces his football under my nose then weaves away. Here are cross-breeds with spray-dyed Zulu pompadours, mini-skirted runaways in grown-up make-up, anorexic androgenes, fatsos in raggedy dark blue. The human form is manifested in such variety you'd think gravity was a different law to each of them.

I remember a scene in *The Caine Mutiny* where Bogart raves

about someone having his shirt out. He wouldn't like it here. Everyone has his shirt out: beachboys, beatles, beatniks, beggars. It's like some fifties beacherama directed by Luis Buñuel and featuring only those sections of the community who *can't* afford cars and surf boards.

'Stop me and make me tell you about my grandchildren,' says a sign round the neck of an obese tramp.

Ominous Hare Krishnas settle like great pink laying-hens on the lawn outside the Life Guard Association where pensioners are playing chess. Genuine destitutes spread their last possessions beside the prom, while effeminate tourists from up the coast glide by on roller-skates. At Muscle Beach the children gawp through railings at seven-stone weaklings laying bare painful new protuberances like martyrs exhibiting wounds. An s/m blonde in studs poses shrieking with an exhausted-looking Popeye. 'OJIBWAY INDIAN CAVE/STATE HISTORICAL MONUMENT' says the sign on a tatty beach bungalow. '*During the early 18th century it was at this spot that the Ojibway Indians held their war councils.*'

A Personal Friend of the Prince of Wales

A mile along the front from Santa Monica is the resort of Venice, home of Alternative LA, where the search is for Selfdom and the transport is by beach-buggy. Even the sea looks different. Wrinkled tinfoil with toy soldiers set in it on stands. Windsails like coloured shark fins. A cigarette hoarding of the Alps tells everyone to COME ALIVE WITH PLEASURE and everyone is certainly trying. A yoga class is being held. Someone yodels to a lyre. Another's head floats in the water. Far off, a tanker is sealed in the afternoon like a little prize.

A crowd has gathered round an old man who is struggling to escape from a mountain of chains. They fall from him and he looks around for a volunteer to be carried across a bed of broken glass.

'How about you, sir?' he says, pointing directly at me.

'No-no,' I tell him, trying to hide my toffee apple, 'I don't . . . I haven't . . .'

'What's the matter, you afraid?'

'No, it's just . . . you know . . . I'm too light for you . . .'

'Ladies and Gentlemen, I believe our volunteer is British. Give him a hand now. Where you frum, sir?'

'London.'

'I'm British myself, you see. I was a personal friend of the Prince of Wales. I showed General Eisenhower how to breathe correctly. You see this ring? Douglas Fairbanks gave me that. Are you satisfied?'

'Not entirely.'

'Ladies and Gentlemen, I shall now carry this young man across the Atlantic Ocean back to his native land . . .'

The ancient picks me up in his flabby old arms and staggers with me towards the bits of broken glass. There is a crunching sound and I shut my eyes lest his naked feet should suddenly absorb what they are supposed to withstand. Dropping my toffee apple, I cling to his shoulder, trying to take some of my own weight. When he has finished he lies down on the glass 'for a rest' and I have to stand on him.

After this horrible experience I need a drink. I sit down at one of the cafés just off the seafront and within minutes my table is covered with personal salvation leaflets.

Sample 1 UNDERSTAND YOUR SEXUALITY by discovering what makes YOU straight gay or 'bi', as revealed through COSMIC TRUTH CONCERNING MAN in 'The Riddle of the Sexes' by 'Asar', author of *Brothers and Sisters in Love*.

Sample 2 JESUS MADE ME KOSHER To me, Judaism was really pretty much the same as Christianity only without Jesus. But I have found that believing in Jesus is the Jewish Thing too. He is our Mashiach (messiah) and our Kaporeh (atonement). Jesus is what makes some of us want to be MORE JEWISH. Ever wonder what MORE JEWISH could mean?

Sample 3 TRY COSMIC BEAM EXPERIENCE A musical sound environment consisting of a 13 ft 300 lb channel strung with steel wire, percussion bells, chimes, gongs and drums, creating a powerful Totality of Healing, Vibrations Massaging the Body Mind & Spirit Inspiring People to Recognise their Inner Potential to Relax Create Feel and BE THEMSELVES.

Sample 4 Consciousness-Raising Dates with Cathy.

Solomon had fled, saying the Charles Manson tribe was after him, so I had a large bare room to myself in Hans's apartment and the unwelcome position of creative-consultant on his motion picture *Rights of Passage*, which was going badly (sic).

'What shall I do?' he would ask, as if something important was about to slip through his fingers. 'The film lacks . . . it lacks . . .'

'I was wondering whether you shouldn't simply turn the birth scene into a trial scene,' I told him. 'You could have Louis XIV as the judge in this all-white hospital-cum-courtroom . . .'

'I don't know . . .'

'Everyone and everything is white, except the infant. Could be visual?'

'Yeah . . . yeah!'

'When the child is born the staff retire to consider their verdict. Flashback to Versailles for the birth-stool scene. Verdict, well, depends how heavy you want to . . .'

'I like it,' Hans would say, suddenly optimistic. 'It presents certain problems, but I think we can use it on a subliminal level . . .'

'You do?'

Then we would get in the Cadillac and drive out to some run-down park in Watts where some black kids were uprooting a slide. Usually I played a priest. Finally I managed to write this priest out of the film altogether and wandered off in search of something to eat: what-on-earth-am-I-doing-here time. There was nothing to eat within miles and the only thing to do seemed to be walking round a stagnant lake or talking to a girl with a Great Dane. The Great Dane had bandaged ears and the girl had bandages on her arm and face. With the pretence of drinking from a stagnant fountain, I asked, 'What happened to his ears?' meaning, 'Did he bite your face and is he going to bite mine?'

'The doctor cut them,' said the girl, allowing the dog to put its paws on my shoulders.

'Why?' I asked, fighting off a tongue like a wet stair lino.

'That's a Great Dane,' said the girl wearily. It looked more like a randy young tapir, but I didn't argue.

'Yes, but why . . . ?'

'They have 'em like that. Didn't you know?'

The dog definitely wanted to go out with me, but the girl couldn't have cared less. I played my last card:

'Oh yes, right, you look like you *both* been in the wars . . . ?'

The girl opened her eyes very wide, then staggered backwards, her arms held stiffly at her sides. I glanced round to make sure no one on the team had witnessed this exchange.

Obviously This Was a Fun Occasion

The Renaissance Faire is a famous tradition in LA. The Earth Shoe classes feel it is something worth fighting for in a colourless world. 'Film For Thy Magick Boxes', 'Terry-the-Tinker Fix-em Everything': the first impression was of Progressive Nostalgia freaks having Mediaeval Fun. Style wouldn't let me have the plan, so I wandered around and got lost among the burlap tents and stalls: slay-the-giant, see-saw jousts, log-fights with bolsters, greasy pigs and greasy poles. It was all rather painfully wholesome, like a big bowl of muesli with only one or two brazil nuts in it to take your mind off your own death. At the Mountebank's Theatre pastiche Shakespeare playlets (comic) alternated with bursts of belly-dancing (serious), a craze which has emerged sideways from the women's movement. These nice Jewish girls looked exactly like desert bedouins: shrieks and pipes and drums. But when a member of the audience took off her top in response she was quickly censored. I complained about the price of a glass of wine and a girl squirted me in the face with some water, leaving me speechless. Another said 'Black what?' when I asked for coffee. They have it 'with' or 'without' over there, for safety.

Obviously this was a 'fun' occasion and one shouldn't carp. But under the back-to-it-all joviality of have-a-go tightrope, climb-the-ladder-and-toot-the-horn, there was a rather thin-blooded atmosphere of intentions having been drawn back from in the interests of propriety and profit. America is cut off from the Middle Ages as surely as it is from the rest of the world, by a thriving New Puritanism. More than anything else at the Faire I remember the mounted Rastaman in dreadlocks and buckskin hovering magnificently on the outskirts like some vestigial image out of *Black Orpheus*.

Paella Can Belly-Roll, Can't You Hon?

I found Style and Amy at the Lucky Dip and we set off across a gulch carpeted with baby frogs. In the car park a wild man called us over to his camper.

'Just like to check out your Duoflex, man,' he said, referring to my box-camera. 'My granny used to own a Duoflex. Where you folks heading?'

'We were just leaving,' said Style.

'Going? Hey! The show don't start till midnight.'

'What are you aiming to do until then?' asked Amy.

'Just about anyone I can lay my hands on, lady,' said the man. 'You folks care to step inside, try a hit a this?'

'You wouldn't care to run us down to Malibu I suppose?' I asked.

'Sure,' said the man, 'step inside.'

Inside the camper was an Oriental rose garden, complete with fountain, stuffed peacock and veiled fatima who fetched us glasses of sweet dark tea. We sat cross-legged on raised Persian carpets, while the man fixed a hubble-bubble. Nobody said anything about this fantasy, so we sipped our tea and talked about the Faire, which our host opined had deteriorated badly in the last few years. No new blood.

'Didn't you like the belly-dancing?' I asked.

'Paella can belly-roll, can't you hon?'

He put on some Kurdish sounds and the fatima commenced belly-rolling until asked to fetch more seed cake.

'Are you people muslims and everything?' asked Amy.

'Dervishes,' said the man, handing me a card which said 'Richard Johnson, Weirdo'.

'How did you get all this into the camper?' asked Style. 'The fountain and everything . . .'

'The fountain works off the cooling pump,' said the man. 'You can't drink it, but we sometimes make tea for visitors. I met Paella in 'Nam. We were studying poetry.'

After about an hour, I asked Richard Johnson if he could run us down to Malibu, as promised.

'I would, see?' he said likeably. 'But we got ourselves this real neat space right here, you know? I run you guys to Malibu I'm gonna lose out, right?'

We set off down the gulch again, crushing froglets at every

step, until a station wagon stopped and we climbed on to a pile of tripods.

'Do you folks smoke marijuana?' asked the couple driving. 'A friend of mine told me this is pretty good stuff.'

This was a Californian joke apparently and everyone was suddenly laughing. Amid mounting paranoia, I asked, 'Is there any angel dust in this?' Nobody answered and eventually Amy said:

'Really, what a time to ask!'

'Why?' I said.

'If you'd had that much dust you'd be tripping outta your skull.'

'You wanna stay offa that stuff till ya know what ya doing, ma freeund,' said the driver, giving me an after-look which I rejected.

By the time they dropped us in Westwood I was feeling so angry I went straight into the Wherehouse and started buying dollar soul deletions again. Style and Amy said they were having dinner somewhere and left. I felt insulted and relieved, but by no means too frightened or tired to do something on my own. I ran after them and asked them to take the records home for me. Then I hit the street.

Julie in Dinosaurs

I walked up and down Westwood for an hour with my eyes on stalks, bought a fancy do-nut to calm myself down, then went back into the record store and watched myself speaking to a girl who apologised to me for flicking my nose with a poster. 'Try not to be weird,' I kept telling myself as I hopped and fussed around her like a gay gallery-owner, then mucked it up by asking her to come over to the 50c rack to tell me about some black guitarist I didn't care about.

'I didn't know they had a 50c rack,' said the girl, turning her back on it and me. At this I gave way to a hollow laugh which went echoing round the store, suddenly waking me to the knowledge that I was thousands of miles from everything that makes life worth living. The girl, I noticed, was talking to the manager about me, but he took no notice, as by that time I was behaving normally again by buying a full-price album by the Flamin' Groovies.

I didn't have to risk anything to pick up Lorri-Lee Rhinehardt and her friend Misty. They were so tranquillised they didn't notice. And they didn't care how the prim citizens of Westwood stared at their mini-skirts. Lorri-Lee seemed to like the same slide music as me, so we went to an expensive bar they both said they knew, where the waitress asked for their IDs.

'Do you think you can handle it?' asked the waitress when large beers were ordered.

'Course,' said Lorri-Lee.

'Where you from?' I asked.

'Hollywood,' said Misty.

'We're actresses,' explained Lorri-Lee. 'Misty was in *Jaws II*. I've done mostly tv promotion work, modelling, you know? I was Julie in *Dinosaurs*.'

'What're you doing now?' I asked. Lorri-Lee and Misty weren't the sort of girls to ask you questions about yourself, even if you *were* foreign.

'Resting,' said Lorri-Lee.

'Drinking,' said Misty.

'In Westwood?'

'They have this big rich student population over here don't they?' said Misty, scouring the bar for talent. 'The people are real snooty round here don't you think? Look at that one. Can I help you mister?'

Quite soon we were asked to leave. There seemed to be no question of goodnights being said, so my only problem was to work out from hints dropped which one I was supposed to be with, although this in itself wasn't worrying me much, as they were both the same.

Then Misty said she would stay on in Westwood and maybe turn a trick at the University, if she could find it. Did she have the Quaaludes on her? She did. Lorri-Lee took some for herself and me and we set off in the direction of Hollywood.

A Riding Accident

The place we went to was some kind of domed reception area in a building off Hollywood Boulevard: desk, telephone, television, stereo, couch, in that order, where Lorri-Lee nevertheless seemed perfectly at ease. I put on the tv and the Elmore James and Lorri-Lee got undressed to it, saying she loved bottleneck.

142

She had a big scar running down her spine, which she said was from a 'riding accident', although it looked as if someone had tried to kill her. Every time I touched this scar, or thought I had, or thought Lorri-Lee thought I had, it was as if a tiny flame was snuffed out inside me and I had to start all over again.

Lorri-Lee wanted to watch the film, so we had to lie on the floor in front of the television. At one point I closed my eyes and tried to blot out the husband-and-wife row going on on screen, the better to trump up a little spurious eroticism for myself. At this moment a loud voice shouted 'Look out, Jim' and my prostate fluttered like an eyelid trying to hold back a tear and I came without her noticing, just as someone in the film was waving a handkerchief to someone from a liner.

'I've just realised I've seen this film before,' said Lorri-Lee, getting up to change channels.

Sign Language

When I got back to the apartment, film cameras had been set up in my room. Hans and Style were asleep in my bed. Sheets hung from the ceiling to indicate an historical setting.

'I'm not gay, you know,' said Hans, coming to the door of the kitchen. 'It's Style. We used to go skinny-dipping together.'

Two hours later, Hans, Style, Jocko and myself were out scouring the barren streets of Watts for a black boy who was supposed to be showing us round a youth club. We finally found him asleep with six other teenagers in a broken down wheel-less caravan. Hans was thrilled. He gave them $5 each not to wake up till he had finished filming them. Our guide was frightened by this. I couldn't understand a word he said, nor could Hans, nor could the guide understand Hans, or me. We used sign language and he ran off. By now the other boys were starting to wake up and cast hungry eyes on Hans's equipment, so we walked swiftly back to the car.

For some reason the rushes showed me asleep in the Cadillac with Hans pointing at a wall. He had white flecks of excitement at the corners of his mouth. The stuff in the caravan didn't come out.

The Life of Brian

My fan Dina Wigg had written to me in England. I was in the shower when she turned up with her boyfriend, a submissive surfie who never once took his eyes off her. Presumably he knew I had asked for her photo. His suspicions were certainly confirmed when I opened the door to them in a towel. An America-compared-to-England conversation now took the place of the wet-scene I had written for Dina and myself, during which I had the impression that I knew more about Los Angeles than they did, although Scott had seen *The Life of Brian* three times and Dina knew all the animals of Ted Hughes.

'It's been real,' said the surfie when they finally left.

Fabulous, We'll Let You Know

To spite Hans, Style took Amy and me to a gallery opening where Amy picked up either Bradford Dillman or Dean Stockwell, whichever one wears the Stetson. Amy popped a piece of cheese into Brad's mouth and Brad invited Amy to a party where Marlon Brando and Robert De Niro were going to be. Amy decently said that I was with her but Style wasn't, so we got into Brad's car and went there.

At the gates a tv camera let us in and we drove through trees to a lake where film business people were standing about, their long shadows reaching back across a lawn to their chauffeur-driven cars. A miniature Taj Mahal gave one the impression of having wandered into one of those idealised gardens painted on the sides of Afghan lorries. The men wore permanent-creased denims, moccasins and gold nuggets and they wove among the women like tiny male angler-fish, seeking anchorage. The women were larger and younger, either lantern-jawed blondes in Turkish Delight top-knots and harem pants, or arabised Jewish women draped in bedouin marriage gifts. Every now and then one of them would throw back her head in mock surrender and give birth to a laugh.

'The most repulsive thing you could ever imagine', Brando once told *Playboy*, 'is the inside of a camel's mouth. It's so awful! That and watching a girl eat small octopus or squid. I mean, I'm not squeamish about anything, I could make an ocarina out of a petrified turd with no problem, but that . . . There's a certain frog that carries its eggs on its back and after they are fertilised, these froglings burst forth from the skin . . . It just makes me sick. I don't like to look at someone's sticky saliva. These people who laugh – ha, ha, ha – and there's a stringer of saliva from their upper tooth to the bottom lip and it bends every time they go ha, ha, it pulsates. Jesus, with one girl, you could take her saliva and walk across the street with it and lay it on the sidewalk and still be connected. The viscosity of some people's saliva is remarkable . . .'

Now there was a man who knew parties.

'I want you to meet Mario,' said Brad, taking Amy high up under the arm and helping her towards the mausoleum.

I wandered around for a few minutes, expecting to meet someone, then I tried to get drunk, but found I was too tired. I picked up a filthy pack of Newport someone had dropped. Then I smoked a Panatella I found stuck in the lips of a statue in the Jacussi. A girl came up and asked if I was on my own, but when she heard I was, seemed to lose interest. There were five of them, she said. In the Jacussi! I lit a Newport and started coughing.

Amy and Brad were talking with Brando, so I went over and got myself introduced.

'Of course, we adore going to London in theory,' somebody was saying.

'That's when it's at its very best,' I said, to a slightly baffled group. I wasn't drunk, but I felt reckless and homesick. I started telling Brando about a friend of mine in whose garden he had once parked his car. This friend of mine was quite interesting, but in the end I had to stop talking about him because there was nothing left to say. At this point Brando looked up and said kindly, 'You like movie stars?' Then one of his aides rescued him by drawing me into conversation about my suit.

'Remember zoot suits?' he said, nudging his colleague.

'Rumble seats?'

'Milk with cream on top?'

'Lavatories with chains?'

'But America is still so fifties,' I said enthusiastically. 'Look at the films, the music, the clothes, the politics. Look at this party. It reminds me of when I was in Australia . . .'

'You from back East?' asked the first aide, fingering my lapel.

'No,' I said. 'I'm . . .'

'My name's Saul,' said a second aide, as if he was going to sock me on the jaw. 'D'you mind my asking how you got in here?'

The British Museum Reading Room

What can you say about the southern Californian countryside? It's the way you think it is. Either you have gum trees lining the road, or you don't. Beyond that it's the desert. Over there are the mountains. Occasionally you get a house, in which case a pubic beard of greenery has sprung up. Life-support systems of all kinds pump sustenance to these desert hide-outs from the four corners of the Third World. Pyramids are very big just now. They use them for 'assertiveness training'. You wear one on your head. It seems they help Californians to have erections. One crank even lives inside a plaster atomic bomb explosion. Now here's a skeleton advertising the race-track. In ten minutes you're back in the suburbs.

My fan Dina Wigg and I had been to see the Henry Moores – grumpy monoliths, positioned in parkland like squires of the manor. These granite abstractions looked set to out-last every other trace of our tacky civilisation. But were we sure we liked what they were saying about us to future generations? No, we weren't sure. We decided we preferred the gloomy shapes of the dinosaurs in McArthur Park.

'Do you like pigs?' asked Dina, who was always thinking about animals.

'Quite, why?'

'I used to work on a pig farm. I go out there sometimes at night. To think, you know? It's peaceful. You wanna go out there?'

'What about Scott?'

'What about him?'

The piggery was the closest I got to country life in America. A nightwatchman shone his torch into Dina's car, then a bar went up and we rattled down a long drive to the piggery, nestling in moonlight. Dina's friend Sue was on night-duty, so it was all right to go in and see the sleeping pigs. The place was constructed like the British Museum Reading Room, with eight rows of stalls radiating from a central control desk. Heavy

146

breathing could be heard against a background of soft music and night-lights.

'You're just in time to help with the turning,' said Sue.

'We have to turn them in the night,' explained Dina, 'otherwise they grow lopsided.'

She gave me a little stick and we went down the rows, tickling the insides of the pigs' ears. Each vast abstraction shook a rudimentary head, looked up in bafflement, then stumbled to its dangerous little legs to check out the food belt. Nothing doing, so it collapsed again into sleep, a movable bar dictating which way. Each pig was encased in a minimum of steel bars, which allowed it just enough room to stand or lie, but not to turn round, as this would have upset the servicing. Fodder was automatically mixed and delivered to the front of each animal on a conveyor belt. Another belt was concealed under a grid at the back. I had a vision of a thousand scholars waiting for the books they had ordered, while the research they produced was borne silently away into the night. There was no question of stepping in anything, said Dina, and I noticed that Sue had on slippers and a clean blouse. The pigs themselves were like clean old men on visiting day: beached, hairless and vague.

'I really love them, don't you?' said Dina, squeezing my hand. 'They're like babies. They smell so sweet don't you think?'

'Don't they mind being this clean?'

'They like it.'

She paused to whisper some words of encouragement to a mountainous beast named Perry Mason. Perry made a snap for her face and I remembered a Hughes poem which warned how they 'chop a half moon clean out, eat cinders, dead cats'.

'What do you see in them?' I asked.

'They're my babies, aren't you, Stella?' said Dina. 'This one's called Chairman Mao. This one's Elvis. You wanna see the conversion room?'

'Not much. What is it?'

We walked round a swimming pool and into an antiseptic chamber with fish-patterned turquoise tiles and low billiard-table lights over a moving rubber draining board. Over the draining board hung several pairs of what looked like heavy-duty head-phones. At the far end were the scalding tanks and the flaying chimneys.

I asked Dina if we were going to her place for a coffee, but she said she had to get up early to train Afghans.

Our New Consultant

'This is Manny,' said Hans, putting his arm round an embarrassed elderly gentleman in rimless spectacles. 'Dr Kohl is our new consultant on the Antipodes.'

'I am happy to meet you,' said the doctor.

The two of them were sitting side by side on the sofa. A large dictionary was open on their laps.

'Dr Kohl is the leading authority on . . . who was it, sugar?' Hans gave the old man a squeeze, as if to get him to speak.

'Patrick White. But I'm not, you know . . . there are many more qualified than, er . . .' He put his hand to his head in search of his back-parting, which had fallen down behind like a goose feather.

'Does this mean you won't be needing me on the film any more?' I asked, trying to keep the excitement out of my voice.

'Of *course* not,' said Hans in outrage. 'We'll still need someone to advise on the popular side, won't we, sugar?' He squeezed the doctor again and looked into his startled old face.

'Er, I hope I haven't, that is . . .' said the doctor.

'Of course you haven't, sugar,' said Hans, winking at me. 'You wanna go to the bedroom now, or what?'

'Who, me?' said the old man, glancing round in alarm.

'Yes, *you*,' said Hans.

'You mean right now?'

'Sure.'

Hans had peeled off his skimpy T-shirt and was posing in the doorway with his Samurai sword. With a single stroke he could have cut off the doctor's anxious, wobbling head.

'Shall I bring this?' asked the doctor, clutching the dictionary to himself like a shield.

'Why not?' said Hans, as he darted up the stairs.

Conqueror and Victim

April rings. Barney has done a bunk. She has to see me. I go round, naturally, but she seems all right again. She has on a red silk sack which is worse than nothing at all. She says Marie-

Georges has been staying with her. Oh yes? How's the foot? Worse? Yes, much. It'll have to come off? I think so.

We have an intense dinner at The Whole Truth, where everyone treats April as if she owned the place. Her beauty, or her dress, have made her a star, a participant. One glance at the back of her head and you know she is one of the tightrope-walking 2 per cent — a race apart, visible and vulnerable, conqueror and victim.

'You have an aura,' I mumble, 'a kind of . . . aura.'

'I know,' she says. 'it's embarrassing . . . that's why I'm so shy.'

I am not taken in by this.

I can't see anything I want on the immense cork menu, except April, so I order a banana split and they have to send out for the banana. This makes April laugh and I go forward a place. She looks at me over her glass and I almost pee my pants.

'Are you a dirty old man?' she asks.

'Yes.'

'Literary types! I had an affair with one in France. You all fancy yourselves as dirty old men. You aren't, but I don't mind. I go along with it. I can handle it, you know what I mean?'

I don't know what she means. I find it hard to imagine other people having any sense of the erotic at all, let alone mine. I take this to be the essence of eroticism. My own starts changing the minute I think anyone is on to it. Is April bamboozling me?

'Promises,' I say.

'Women have more courage than men, that's all.'

'Maybe, but you have a fail-safe. In the end men feel responsible for you.'

'Rubbish!'

'If a girl has the balls to go up to a man, nine times out of ten he won't put her down. He has balls himself and he knows how it feels to be kicked in them.'

April disagrees. She says the female experience is THE new experience. No one can help them. Does she want help, I wonder? I ask the waiter for the bill, but when it comes it is so big I have to pay by traveller's cheque and go back ten places. I ask for a puppy-bag for April's untouched steak and go back another ten. By now I am almost out of the game, but April lets me win at the last moment by taking my arm as we leave the restaurant. That, after all, is what it's all about.

I missed Dina's dog-show, but we met for drinks afterwards, 'to say goodbye'. Scott was away on Retreat with the 'Cult of the Lamb', she said, leaving me to draw my own conclusions about this. From 'The Funky Warrior' to her bedroom took six and a half hours, but it seemed like an eternity. In the bar, I thought the clock had stopped at a quarter past ten.

Dina's fondness for animals had started on holiday in the Adirondacks, she told me, just after her father had disappeared. She'd found a lemming who had missed the annual suicide dash because of snake-bite. She'd nursed it with a fountain pen, then it had run off. She'd written a poem about it. After that she got interested in poetry and had one accepted by the World Wildlife Fund. She'd written to me when she saw my poem about cats. But why had I asked for her photo? Dina's outdoor breasts stood there in front of me like chubby schoolboys, patiently forming and dissolving under a T-shirt of the World Wildlife Fund, waiting for my answer. I managed to stop myself from telling them and we went back to her apartment at the kennels. Once inside this haven, we spent another aeon passing cultural knick-knacks back and forth to one another across her coffee table, while hounds bayed downstairs.

'You ever seen one of these?' she'd ask, handing me an inflated deep-sea angler fish, covered with prickles. 'How about this?' – a model of a famous ballerina made out of dried civet. 'Or this?' – the shrunken head of a man from North Borneo. I batted them all back to her as fast as I could, then she got the idea that I wanted to see something more literary.

'Hey, you like Michelangelo?'

'Sure.'

'This book . . . see . . .'

'God!'

'Isn't it incredible?'

'Amazing.'

'I mean, the *poems* . . .'

'Incredible.'

I give the OK to another exhausting compilation and pass it back to Dina for re-shelving. When I sit beside her on the mattress, she says 'Hi.'

'Hi,' I say.

'Hey, you mind my asking one thing?'

'No, go ahead.'

'Are you, you know, clean and everything?'

I don't know about this, but I reassure her and she looks relieved and goes ahead and puts on the Rolling Stones. So much for Michelangelo. In her bathroom are rows of vaginal purgatives, in spearmint and other flavours. Are these supposed to be invisible, I wonder, or am I supposed to choose one? When I come back into the room, Dina is already naked. She is busy lighting a candle in the form of a frog.

A Perfectly Logical 'No'

All right, I called April again. She said: what, are you still here? I said I was and she wanted to know what I was doing. I said I wasn't doing anything. If I wasn't doing anything, she said, I must be leaving. This had never struck me, but it seemed correct. I said I was leaving the next day, so she said come to dinner.

When I got there I noticed the place had changed. It looked run-down and dirty and April was wearing sandals. A girl called Zoe had moved in, with her maid Nadia, a film extra. Also present for the evening was Jim, a Texas curio dealer, interested in rare bibles. Jim seemed to have been invited for my benefit, as he had been to England. Zoe said since she'd been in LA she'd found it possible to have valuable relationships with women, especially April, whose accountant she had become. Nadia thought so too. I asked how you value a relationship and Zoe said men were so formal. Jim had something in his pocket which he wanted Zoe to sign on behalf of April, so he agreed with Zoe. He was a smooth, one-up business bore, who knew more about everything than anyone, except Zoe. At first he said 'It's a trip.' Australia, punk rock and Copenhagen china were all 'a trip'. Later, when he had had too much to drink and spilled his coffee on the paper, still unsigned, he started mumbling 'It's a bummer,' which was a better description of the evening.

The maid Nadia cooked us a shoddy little meal, then we went out 'on the town'. We were going to the Gypsy Caravan, but first it was over to Danny and Benny's place for cocaine.

Once high, we spent many useful moments gazing at Danny's production of varnished animal cracker brooches. A possible career for Danny? Everyone seemed to hope so, especially Benny, who raised his eyes to heaven for my benefit. How would I like to have one?, said Danny. I could have eaten a handful easily, but Danny wanted me to choose one, then wear it to the nightclub.

'Which one would you like?' he said.

'I like the camel.'

'Well, see, there's only one camel . . .'

'I'll take the cat.'

'Take the dog.'

April blew me a tremendously sultry kiss and I started to relax, believing that I might get one delivered personally later, although if I was April I'd be happy enough just walking down the street in one of those sacks.

At the Gypsy Caravan Zoe wanted to teach Nadia the tango, with me as the man, or the woman rather, but Nadia wouldn't look. She thought the Caravan was 'dumpy' and couldn't see anyone she recognised there. Finally Zoe flung me on the floor and Nadia said, 'I know a great gay disco!' So we went there. In the car Zoe explained to everyone that the reason nobody could do the tango was that they weren't black.

'Music has a lot to do with the senses,' she said, 'you know what I mean? Feeling.'

'Feeling,' I said. 'What's that?'

'Well, you said it, buster.'

At the gay disco I danced with April, but April danced on her own, adjusting her camera angles for someone in the restaurant upstairs. I said, 'If I say you have a beautiful body will you hold it against me?' I couldn't think of anything else to say. The nice answer is Yes. April gave a perfectly logical 'No', danced close for three and a half seconds, then wanted another tequila sunrise. Jim was dancing with Zoe. He said 'It's a bummer' and passed out at the table. 'What a clinker!' said Nadia.

When I got the three girls back to their door we all stood there at cross purposes for a moment. I was supposed to be saying 'Farewell', but I said, 'Well, what's to become of me then?'

'What do you mean, what's to become of you?' said April.

'Look,' said Zoe triumphantly, 'why don't we just go on

up and leave you two to work this one out between you, OK?'

'All right, Zoe, you go on up,' I said.

'Now, what are you talking about?' said April.

'I was just wondering what happens to me now,' I said. 'Why don't you come to my place?'

'What happens to you?' said April. 'I'll tell you what happens to you, you go back to England, that's what happens to you.'

'Really?'

'Yes.'

She made me a cup of coffee and we stood in the kitchen making last-minute gestures at a map of New York State. Then April put out her cigarette and offered me her perfectly formed cheek. I kissed it and went back to England.

I felt like making myself walk all the way back to the apartment in my horrid pointed boots, but I managed to pick up a bus. The apartment was deserted. My own stuff was lying on the floor, but everything else had gone, even the boomerangs. I got on the phone to my family to tell them I was leaving for New York the next day. My daughter answered the phone. 'Daddy, you sound American,' she said. 'Do you sleep with girls?' 'Of course not,' I said.

8

THE NORTHERN ROUTE EAST

No Getting Down

Now the film has been exposed to the Californian light I have to wind it back to New York in the cramped camera of this bus. I feel the sadness of having turned my back on the Pacific, of being headed east again, of having seen America. I'm dreading it, but I have a reading to do in Boston. If you want to you can skip all the discomfort and go straight back to New York and Vicky. After all, what are books for, I'd join you, but . . .

I see the one attractive girl in the bus is already paired with a late-arriving young hunter in single shoulder patch and binoculars. He lets her look through them and they see the same thing. A pity.

I have Cliff and his sister Tania, teenagers whose breaking up parents have packed them off with sandwiches to live with an aunt in Salt Lake City. He handsome, protective, precocious, asking me questions about my background and saying 'Majestic!' to everything, she tired and old and weepy at fourteen, looking up to him who's going to be a statesman and a foreign correspondent some day.

Yucca Flats. Trees like madmen.

'Looks like they don't believe in getting too close to one another,' says Cliff.

Is that a little mountain community up there, pine trees shading down a ravine? In Europe it would be, but here it's a sulphur mine with smoke standing in marble columns against blue, the miners housed in trailers near the mobile gas unit and the company flag of a six-shooter.

'Majestic!' says Cliff as a white-padded and green button-upholstered speed launch called 'Geronimo' slowly overtakes our bus on its trailer.

A life-size head waiter welcomes us to Death Valley, 'Watch Downhill Speed', where hot-dogs, cold beer and rest room are available at 'The Depot', but 'No getting down,' says Driver Ponting, going inside himself. In the window are home-made models of cacti and wildcats for sale, in imitation of the big town souvenir chains. 'Help Wanted' says a sign, as raggedy children dash in and out and the woman dries her hands to deal with the gas pump.

'That just *has* to be America,' says a new woman sitting next to me. 'All they need is some rattlesnakes in a cage some-where . . .'

I Touched Him and He Gave Me His Pamphlet

The sun setting now for the first of our four nights on the road. It lights the mountains ahead with a torch beam, the ranges set one behind the other, each paler and taller than the one before, crazy-man trees standing out like deranged Indians. The country station plays soft, but there's nothing really nothing to turn off. . .

'Let me see if I can tell where you come from by your accent.' says the new woman, waking me. 'Canada, am I right?'

'England.'

'*England*? You know Andrew Culver well?'

'Would that be Michael Culver's brother by any chance?'

'No, Culverwell. He came to Dallas last year. He sings for God. He was so beautiful. He had on this kind of pink ruffle shirt and a maroony burgundy jacket. Don't you know his "I Believe in Him"? I went up to him afterwards and just said "Right on, brother". I touched him and he gave me his pamphlet. England must be a beautiful place. Look, give me your address. Let me send you a book called *Understanding Each Other*.'

I give her my address and she says she is going to pray for me and my wife if I pray for her and Bob. I pray for her and Bob and she falls asleep beside me and I never see her again.

Months later, my wife received a letter from this woman. 'Hi,' it said,

> we have yet to meet but I know you from afar. You were there with Hugo and me in the bus that night, our minds and hearts grappling with acceptance, challenge and love for the strange and unknown. My weary body quit trying and escaped into the dark haven of rest. I seldom give up when my heart leaps to loving someone who reaches out to others. And so it is feeling frustrated that I knew NOT how to love Hugo, as with Mary Magdalene I sing 'I don't know how to love Him', altho I know Hugo and I have different tastes in music. I wonder about your tastes? I dance by the hour to Neil Diamond's 'Hot August Night' and 'Jesus Christ Superstar'. You? This comes on the wings of Cherubims and Seraphims, from me and Jesus. (Have you heard Andrew Culverwell play and sing his own music God gives him?)

'Funny people you pick up,' said my wife, handing me the letter.

The Oasis Bar, Slots 'n Pool

After a neck-snapping night it's good to be awake again. The scenic backdrop swoops upwards from hallucinatory wagon trains toiling for ever west. Buzzards wheel over Calico, a ghost town reconstruction, now abandoned. The map rolling up quickly now. You flatten it out so carefully going west, then you turn around and it rolls up suddenly on its own and you're back where you started.

The girl's name is Jackie. Her companion is Keith. We exchange magazines. The *Reno Round-up* has a

BACHELORETTE OF THE WEEK

Women dislike me because of my popularity with their husbands. As a professional dancer they would throw their drinks over me. When I was dancing some of the girls danced nude, but with class. It looked good and was sensuous. Other girls made dancers look like bitches. Some clubs make girls spread themselves open. It's things like that have ruined the art of dancing. I was brought up religiously. I enjoy cooking,

156

sewing and entertaining friends. I guess that makes me a natural for my job as a cocktail waitress at The Golden Spike. In my spare time I exercise and do charity work. I also love animals.

At the Nevada-Utah border they have a last-ditch casino, The Oasis, a big shed near the bus depot where you can waste your last dollar before the Mormon state sets in. At eleven in the morning it's an animated hangover. They have a 'Four-Strong Song Team With Comedy' called The Bunkers, who play and talk very slowly so they can go on all day and night. The humour is so etiolated it makes you feel faint. One passenger wandered in half asleep, thinking it was the souvenir shop, and accidentally won $50 on the Venus Probe. He was immediately surrounded by Easy Rider-style beggars asking for loose change. I had the impression of Middle Eastern chaos suddenly miraging out of the desert and checked my address book.

'We're rather short, thanks,' I tell a sun-scarred Abe Lincoln in plaits as I tear myself away from the hypnotic Gift World and return to the bus. After travelling on Greyhound for a while you get the feeling they are merely ferrying you from one souvenir outlet to the next, with only the postcard rack and the town's name on the water tower as variables.

Ride Them Little Dawgies

Jackie didn't sleep last night so I offer her my double seat. She doesn't want it, but Keith says 'OK, I don't care' and stretches out in it while I talk to Jackie about his hunting trip to the Yukon. He has a special big gun for caribou, she explains. Jackie too has travelled. Do I know James Taylor at all? We say what we think about adultery, vivisection and Pop. Then it's Salt Lake City, 'High School Graduation Kung Fu Demonstration Today.' We all walk down the street to Sambo's, where the only black man shows us the Mormon temple like a cake from Disneyland, iced-in from behind with snow-topped mountains. We buy religious postcards with little bags of salt for taking a pinch of.

Keith approaches with a local drink for me. What's this, Keith, a beaker full of the warm South, or a glass of your pee? It tastes like spearmint vindaloo. I didn't know he cared about Jackie . . .

'Thanks Keith, you must be Canadian, right?'

'Right, man. How did you guess?'

Cliff buys Tania a ring and they go off into their life. Jackie buys a white beret and I take her photograph. I tell her, 'You may be the best damn girl in this whole country,' and she hitches up her skirt. Over her shoulder I see a familiar face. My God, it's Johnny! The con from Williamsburg, the one who wanted to manage me. He looks ten years older, but he's still talent-spotting I see – rolling up his sleeve for a pair of Mormons in neckties, who look horrified at the sight.

'Johnny!' I say, in spite of myself. 'It is Johnny, isn't it?'

'Huh?'

'Williamsburg? *You* remember. On the bus!'

'Williamsburg?' say Johnny. 'Well, how ya doing Williamsburg? Take a shot a this. You don't look so good.'

I take some of the Dewar's, knowing I have no choice. But Johnny's eye has lighted on Keith.

'Who's your friend, Williamsburg?'

'This is Keith. Keith, Johnny.'

'Pleased to meet you, Keith. Keith looks like a man who could handle himself in an emergency, am I right?' He forces the Dewar's into Keith's unwilling hands. 'I like your jacket, Keith.'

He takes his protégé outside and they look at the mountains through Keith's binoculars. I see Johnny holding up a monstrous forefinger, which seems to hypnotise the youth. Then they get on the bus together.

Later, Johnny tells us he is going to take Keith to a ranch where he used to castrate bullocks. 'Ride them little dawgies, eh Keith?' Keith's eyes are bulging out of his head, but he wants to go there. He thought he was going to Denver with Jackie, now he's going to Cheyenne with a criminal. This is no bad thing.

'Mind if I borrow these?' says Johnny, putting Keith's binoculars round his neck.

The Silent Type

A winding quarry leads out of Salt Lake Valley into a jade sunset. Hours of headbanging sleeplessness and cold give way to morning on the Green River, high in the Wyoming Rockies, the Quaker state, where all they have is sky and the occasional white dart of a B52 rehearsing its figure-skating — a scratch fanning to skid-marks by the time we stop for breakfast and souvenirs at Hoppie's Hangout: 'Dance to The Polka Kings — Waltz-Polka-Modern'. Across the road a huge urn waits outside a laid-back undertaker's called Vase Funerals.

In the Rock Springs rest room is an erotica dispenser: pep-pills, puzzles, prophylactics. 'Learn Anatomy The Fun Way with Torrid Terri's Cutie Nudie Puzzle No. 3. Just Slide in My Pieces'. I put in 25c for a 'Date-Getter (Guaranteed)'. 'It works automatically,' says the packet. 'You don't have to say a word. Don't be alone tonight or any night. Join the peppy generation with a Pocket-piece Charmer. The Secret to Social Success.' Inside is a printed metal disc:

I am the Silent Type. Any chance to crawl into the sack with you tonight. If so keep this token if not please return it.
(Please see other side)
I'm not as good as I once was but I'm as good once as I ever was. PS You don't have to say yes just smile.
(Hong Kong)

When we get back to the bus I hand this to Jackie, who passes it to Keith, who smiles at me. Johnny says he can't read. He certainly can't smile. His face is drawn tight like scar-tissue. He looks as if he needs the blood of a virgin urgently. He takes a lonely pull on the Dewar's.

How Strange To Be Travelling

A new driver, always balding, climbs in bright and fresh at Laramie, Wyoming, slots in his bright new name: R. K. Hyde, Safe Reliable Courteous. 'Break it up in back there, boys. No drinking now.'

And so it continues to unroll, this back-projection America: table-tops, trailer-towns, archaic hoardings, 'Chew Mail Pouch Tobacco', picnic shelters like giant As go 'AAAAA' across the Red Desert, Wyoming, bandy cowboys fossilised in the reptilian stillness. The only movement comes from the drinking-bird wells, hesitating then plunging. The only trace of

159

modern America appears in the wacky cigarette ads pleading with the skeletons of cattle: 'The Box' (Winston), 'The Turk' (Camel), 'Come to Marlboro Country'. Well, this is it I suppose, if it's anywhere. I want to like it all, and I do, but it's difficult to get comfortable and I have a piece of the desert in my eye.

The body is a blindfold to the traveller. You see everything through a haze of tiredness and pain. You wonder what you're doing there. I had a postcard from Philip Larkin years ago, forwarded to me in India. 'How strange to be travelling,' he said. 'I left the UK for four days in 1951, I think it was; before that it would be 1937. Don't you miss the cricket scores? or the Ward trial reports?' The word 'travel' is the same as the word 'travail', meaning labour. It comes from the latin *trepalium*, an instrument of torture involving three wooden stakes.

At Cheyenne we all stroll downtown and try on dark blue cowboy boots tipped with lizard. I find an old Lee Dorsey album. A man in souvenirs says he used to pay Indians a silver dollar for arrowheads. Now he gives them a beer for fakes. Johnny has a word with him and he gives Johnny a hundred dollars for Keith's binoculars. We leave Keith and Johnny at the Eat 'n Run Gas-o-Mart, arguing about a car.

Rapist Swallows Alarm Device in Mystery Terror Dive

I'm sitting in the bus wearing a blue track suit top and reading a story in the *Omaha World News* about a murderer-rapist last seen on a bus wearing a blue track suit top. Jackie looks shocked, but says it couldn't possibly be me. 'Police are still scratching their heads,' goes another story, 'about the latest business to hit St Louis, where prostitution and sexual massage are illegal. For $30 an hour an attractive scantily clad woman will read a so-called dirty book to a customer. That's all. Both persons sit in straight back chairs. The place is called The Reading Room. It advertises in local papers and its telephones are frequently busy, say Police.'

Country changing from the high barren Great Divide to the lusher prairies of Nebraska, a different, older America emerging in this central space of emptiness and road. At night there is even more of it. Omaha and Des Moines are places I will remember sheathed in star-laden darkness and cold, a breath of ice-dry air coming to my lungs from another planet, as I walk down a deserted street in Omaha.

If It's Midnight, This Must Be America

The black night-guard in the all-new Des Moines bus station saunters among the sleeping travellers like a gaoler of dreams. Screens flicker with abstruse knowledge. Names of places I have been to and not been to flood over me as I work out where I am: Modesto, El Paso, New Orleans, reminding me of tiredness and longings. If it's midnight, this must be America, where everyone *except* tourists has an American accent and knows how to operate the vending machine. 'All Aboard for Chicago.' The same camp but winsome voice follows you wherever you go on the buses, flinging out coded clues to your future, politely moving you on to where you must go, 'And thanks for going Greyhound.' He must be the most influential man in America.

Trial by Sleep

At last Jackie's sleeping head falls from my shoulder to my chest and from there on to my lap. My own head on the block now till 7 a.m. I smash it against the window all night, fall asleep as we get down for a meal at somewhere like Iowa. You're in the last stages of exhaustion, you stagger to the station for a little peace and sustenance. What do you find? The Gift Court. The Amusement Center. The Cocktail Lounge and Gottlieb's Outer Space: 'It's More Fun To Compete!' You feel your way to the restaurant. 'Get in Touch With America,' rejoices the menu, 'Go Greyhound.' 'Get Out of the Ordinary, Go Navy,' implores something else. Opposite you sits a giant teddy bear from the shooting gallery. This is sleep-walker's America, trial by travel. At Iowa City I feel as if I'm coming up for air for the last time, my head bandaged with broken glass, my feet bound by the vibrations of a '16-wheel Stratocruiser'.

'You wanna party?' says a cruising hooker.

'I am partying, thanks.'

Enough is enough. I can't face another night of this and I persuade Jackie she can't either. We will find a hotel in Chicago and 'get some sleep at last'.

How to Grow a Shrubbery

'I keep this room for friends,' says the Greek manager of the Astor Hotel as he shows us how the water comes and goes and no shower for only $20. From the bed we can see the massive Greyhound symbol on the station wall opposite, cars parked on the roof, a skyline of gold-topped skyscrapers and overhead trains. At long last we have left forecourt America and can see real streets again, shops up against the sidewalk, people walking. The bed's like a rowing boat, so what?

Unfortunately Jackie can't enjoy the sluttishness of one-night cheap hotels. Normality is her element, so the excitement is tuned to tv level as she concentrates on 'How to Grow a Shrubbery'. She puts on her nakedness like armour and rubs herself with baby oil as if she was cleaning windows. 'They're wearing *us*,' said Marshall McLuhan when he was taken to a topless restaurant.

I see The Manhattans are playing, so we go out for some fun. Orange and pink suits on State Street. Lemon trousers and white jackets. Everyone in hats. Porters in red caps. Black children in curlers, their hair bleached here and there. Music in the air. I pick up the *Walking the Dog* album by Rufus Thomas. My handicap is now ninety LPs. This great dark town is as good as New York. I wouldn't mind working here.

We Didn't Even Have the Fresh Catfish

When Playmate Connie Kreski leased her own apartment on the outskirts of Detroit, she and her girlfriend Mimi and their escorts for the day rented a truck and proceeded to make the big move. After a few hours of packing, Connie said, 'I hadn't realised just how much stuff I managed to accumulate over the years until I tried getting it all together.' When Connie arrives at her new address, date 'Larry gives her a helping hand with housewares (right), before he and Paul begin hauling in the more formidable furnishings. 'My friends couldn't have been more helpful,' says Connie. 'They worked from noon until after dark, not stopping till everything I brought was put away.' (*Playboy* caption)

This morning Jackie is not altogether happy about her night

of sin. She's missing her dog and wants to move on. 'I didn't get off on that city,' she tells me haughtily.

As the bus pulls out I think I see Johnny talking to the uniformed station attendant, but decide I am mistaken. Jackie too thinks it was him. No sign of Keith.

'Folks, this is the highest point of the Skyway,' announces the driver as we take the elevated section over old Chicago. 'And once again to your left you see the southern tip of Lake Michigan, Queen of the Sea Buffet, Mr Cadillac and Bob's Talk of the Town . . .'

To the right we see an incredible industry-scape of persecuted rivers, boats and chimneys, the whole scene charged with apocalyptic gloom, partly due to the semi-smoked windows through which one is invited to take in 'GREYHOUND'S AMERICA. SEE IT ALL. SEE IT CLOSE'.

'I taught there was an observation dome,' says an elderly woman in a T-shirt with clouds on it, sitting across the aisle from us. 'Don't they bring you no blankets or nuthin? I usually fly you know. They got a foot-rest or what?' She complains about someone smoking 'during the flight'.

Jackie sees a dead mammal lying curled up round a tyre in a truck yard and she cries. I show her the dead armadillo crammed into the cloud-lady's basket and she laughs. Then she cries again, saying we didn't even have the fresh catfish.

Crawling round Atlanta Looking for Board Games

In the rest room at Toledo a perfectly respectable man is sitting on the basin in his underpants, washing his feet. He looks as if he has a perfect right to behave like this, which, in America, he has. Anyone has in fact, unless any vital commercial interests are being jeopardised:

FIRING OVER LEG-HAIR ON WAITRESS UPHELD
The right of a restaurateur to fire a waitress who refused to shave her legs has been upheld by the Connecticut Commission on Human Rights and Opportunities. The Commission ruled against Judith Quist, who said she had not shaved her legs for five years.

At Cleveland Jackie has to split for Buffalo. I try to persuade her to come to Atlantic City, but she says it is called Atlanta and 'too risky'. I explain to her what it is – the six-mile board-walk, the seafront, the few streets which give their names to the original Monopoly. But she says Monopoly is 'too obsessive'. She doesn't like the sound of it. I try telling her what I like about B-movie, back-lot America and she says I am sick. I suppose it's the same as Americans saying how 'quaint' London is. She says Real Americans haven't got time to go crawling round Atlanta looking for board games. They have to earn a living. 'That's the Main Feature, you know.'

At Cleveland station Jackie squeezes my face and says 'Smile!' which annoys me. That's no way to get anyone to smile, I tell her. We look for a bar to make up in, but can't agree on one, so Jackie gets an earlier bus and we wave thankfully to one another through the plate glass. I had better phone Vicky.

On the Theology Side

Another sleepless night in bedlam. The cloud-lady complains about my radio. My new partner, an enormously fat 'Amer-ican' American, says he saw her eating with *chopsticks* in Cleve-land.

'She's an odd fish,' I say.

'She's a communist,' he opines.

'Really?'

'English are you?'

'Yes.'

'Not Jewish?'

'No.'

'England goes down we all go down.'

'Exactly.'

'On the theology side England gave us the King James Version. That's our recipe book. We get a Jewish president he's gonna change the language to Hebrew.'

'You must be joking!'

A short nap and he wants to know if I think fatness is more acceptable in Europe. He says the communists and Jews are driving him out of his native land. Then he gives me the recipe for Green Goddess dressing: anchovy paste, sour cream, parsley, spring onions, sugar, vinegar, salt, spices. He can't remember the proportions.

164

In Pittsburgh everyone piles out of the bus half asleep and gathers round the *Playboy* and *Penthouse* section of the souvenirs stall. One person holds a copy open, while the rest of us look over his shoulder. It is worth seeing. The stall also sells caps, peeing monks and praying hands in clear plastic:

> Have faith in your country
> Have faith in your land
> Have faith in your soul
> And you will have faith in your hand

It's Full of Crazies Up Here

The cloud-lady is confused about lockers. I show her how she can get both her cases in a 25c locker. She changes her mind and puts them in a 50c locker, saying her daughter can afford it, she's got five kids and her husband has an accountant.

I queue for the phone and there's a man in there hitting the glass. He says he's got to get to New York this weekend or he's going to kill people. 'It's full of crazies up here,' he says. 'There's one here just looking at me. He's been following me since Toosday . . .' He pulls back his jacket and there's a sheath knife on his belt. Shaken, I get on a bus going to Los Angeles. After a minute I realise what I have done and the driver has to stop to let me down. I run around the streets of Pittsburgh in a panic. When I get back to the station I find there's time for a meal. Am I refreshed? Do I want to be refreshed so thoroughly at 3 a.m.? Better than the sleep torture maybe. But the people look shifty now, approaching New York. The cloud-lady claps her hands.

The Spot for Mature Party People

Daylight and Paterson. Vicky isn't in. I speak to Marvin. Good old Marvin! How are you? Really? Oh, I'm sorry to hear that. Fucking dealers, right. I'll see you later, OK? Marvin has been sold some marjoram again . . .

Bridges hump in the distance out of dead land, New York across fields, a clear space between the Empire State and the Trade Center, my heart beating faster. Ten minutes later a whole section of the city shows up, in colour this time as the day gets going, the giant anthills of Manhattan growing out of a suburb on a bank. Now the bus seems to dawdle for hours in the gap which opens up before arrivals. One more great suspension bridge and we are thrust forward into the present at last.

Where are the New Jersey Disco Crowd?
They're still at The Metal Brook,
the Spot for Mature Party People.

I wonder where Vicky is though.
Bags full of sixties soul albums weighing a ton again this bus-lag morning. I order the child's menu by mistake at Wargreen's Coffee Counter and the waitress looks round for an audience for this cream-puff. I take a coffee and she says drink it today, feller. Hello New York!

9
STAYING WITH VICKY

Simon Has Some Kind of Allergy, Plus He Breeds Alsatians

At the Kennington there was a nickel from Vicky and a note
saying to call her. She was going to visit friends in White Plains,
did I want to come? They were really nice people, she said, but
slightly strange: Marthe, Simon and a dog called Orville.
When we arrived, Marthe seemed to be waving goodbye to us
from her bedroom window. She had had a great many opera-
tions, Vicky said. We went into the kitchen and saw the pretty
maid watching tv in her bra. Later, Marthe came down and we
all made ourselves cups of tea and carried them through into
the living room, where nothing much happened for two hours.
Marthe was trying to relax, she said. Finally, Simon came
storming in from his ride, dripping with sweat and shouting
about the 'Administration'. He had to talk to Marthe upstairs
about her next operation, he said.

'Did you know I had an extra kidney now, Vicky?' asked
Marthe.

'Of course Vicky knows that,' said Simon.

They left the room together and Vicky told me that they
didn't have much of a sex-life on account of the scars.

'I saw them when I was in depression last fall,' she said, 'and
it didn't do me a damn bit of good.'

'What scars?' I asked.

'Marthe had two kids by Caesarean section. She was only
supposed to have one.'

'Where are they, the kids?'

'I don't know. You never see them. I don't think they live here. Simon has some kind of allergy, plus he breeds Alsatians.'

Simon and Marthe came back into the room. Marthe had her hands over her face.

'It's passover tomorrow,' she said. 'Mom's coming over and I haven't got anything ready yet. What shall I do? I haven't even bought the seder. Now the shops are closed.'

She sat down on her husband's knee.

'Don't worry hon,' said Simon. 'Julie can ask one of her friends. Everything will be all right. Now. Who's going to help with the search?'

I thought he meant for the passover meal, but it was for the unwanted leaven. At about ten o'clock on the morning of the passover all the leaven that has remained in the house, together with all the leaven collected during the search the previous night, is ceremonially burned. It is customary to place a few bits of leaven here and there so that when the search is made some leaven is found – otherwise the benediction recited before the ceremony would be in vain.

The maid was told to get dressed and off she went to try and find some stuff for the seder. The rest of us carried out the search. We looked in vases, under mats and behind the laundry basket in the shape of a begging dog. Under the bed in the spare room was a small saddle. Simon had been around and left a few crusts here and there and I found one under my own chair. After the leaven had been gathered and gift-wrapped in blue polythene, the following was said: 'Any leaven that may still be in the house, which I have not seen, or have not removed, shall be as if it did not exist, and as the dust of the earth.'

Next, the maid came back, saying she couldn't find anyone in, but she thought one shop was open in the morning. She'd get up early and see.

'Thanks, Julie. You're a saint,' said Marthe.

No Magic Cubes? I'll Kill Myself

Marthe's divorced mother was visiting from hospital, where she was on the critical list, she said. She was dressed from head to toe in white buckskin. She seemed to take an instant liking to me and ignored everyone else in the room.

'You Jewish, Hugo?'

'No. I'm sorry.'

'Don't apologise. Why you apologise?'

'No, it was a joke.'

'A JOKE?' Silence.

'I heard this Russian Jew being interviewed on the radio this morning,' I said, failing to change the subject. 'He'd just arrived in Vienna and they were asking him what he wanted to do in America and he said he wanted to work with dolphins in Miami Beach.'

Marthe's mother looked at me in open admiration.

'It doesn't matter what Englishmen say to me,' she said, 'I just think anything they say is so brilliant and fantastic because of the way they say it.'

'A lot of them change their minds, apparently, when they get to Vienna,' I said. 'They ask to go back to Russia.'

'You've forgotten the magic cubes again, Marthe,' said Simon.

'No magic cubes?' said Marthe. 'I'll kill myself.'

'Not till after the seder, dear, please, for my sake,' said her mother.

'What seder?' said Simon under his breath.

After conferring, the family agreed that I could stay for the passover feast. I didn't want to, but I seemed to have no choice. Vicky was staying the night. She hadn't told me that.

'I'm not putting you on the same floor,' said Marthe, showing us to rooms at opposite ends of the house. 'It's my old-fashioned principles.'

The Bitter Herb

In the morning a Mobile Passover Trailer called at the house. With the Passover Packs came a number of printed cards which we propped against our glasses on the table:

1 Recite the Kiddush
2 Wash the hands
3 Eat a green vegetable
4 Break the middle Matzah and hide a half of it for the Afikoman
5 Recite the Passover story
6 Wash the hands

7 Say the Hamitzi and the special blessing for the matzah
8 Eat a bitter herb
9 Eat the bitter herb and the matzah together
10 Serve the festival meal
11 Eat the Afikoman
12 Say the grace after the meal
13 Recite the Hallel
14 Conclude the seder

It took about an hour to get even as far as the bitter herb and everyone's tummy was rumbling. Simon was in a black mood about the 'Administration', but he cheered up when he heard that his father-in-law in Miami was going to have the prostate operation.

'It's my opinion that that particular operation is the best reason so far invented for putting an end to it all prematurely,' he said, drawing a finger across his throat.

Vicky's Climax

Marvin still couldn't pay his rent, so Vicky let me have his room while I was in New York. Marvin couldn't tell the difference. In theory, he had the day-bed. In practice he stayed in his old room, stoned, and I got to sleep in the bed if and when he ever went to work.

One morning Vicky wandered in in her dressing gown, wielding an aerosol, of which she had many. She killed a few flies, then got into bed with me, brushing the sheet and checking the time on her watch.

'How long have we got?' I asked.

'I had a letter from Zak,' she said. 'You wanna read it?'

'Not much.'

The letter was scarred from long folding. I started to read about money, journeys, drugs, apartment houses, and tight-fisted relatives of Vicky's who were 'off the wall'.

'I ever tell you about the first time I had an orgasm?' she asked, showing me her tremendous teeth. 'Like a man I mean.'

'Like a man? How come?'

'I was writing to this old friend of mine, telling her about Zak and the new house and everything. Peter was there, rehearsing.

Peter's my best friend. He's gay. You'll really like him. He writes beautiful poems. He's coming round Thursday I think it is . . .'

'Yes, but . . .'

'Anyway, Peter asked me what I was writing and when I told him he said to read it out loud. I was lying on my tummy and while I was reading Pete put his hand between my legs, like this. I stopped reading, thinking he wanted to screw or something, but he told me to keep right on, not to move . . .'

Without a single break in her running commentary, Vicky had shed her dressing gown and got underneath me. I thought, so long as she doesn't stop talking suddenly, this could be it.

'I didn't think much about it,' she said, 'but the tension must have been building up inside me without my realising it. I mean, I didn't really have *time*, you know, to get *ready* for what happened, to make *way* for it. Pete just kept telling me to *read*, so that when the moment came . . . when the moment came . . .'

When the moment came, the door burst open and Marvin came dashing back into the room, having forgotten something for work.

'Sorry, you guys,' he said. 'I just gotta find . . . something . . . important down here . . .'

I was aware of this stoned left eye winking at me from very close as he rummaged around under his bed for his grass.

'Ahhh . . .' he said at last, as he found what he was looking for.

'Marv-hon,' said Vicky, 'be a doll and drop off my laundry for me would you, hon? It's in the hall, the garbage too if you've got a hand. Don't forget it's your turn to do out the john . . . we need soap for the dishes . . . Sean left his deodorant behind . . .'

Marvin slipped out of the room.

'Anyway,' said Vicky, 'Pete just told me to keep on reading, and when the climax came it took me completely by *surprise*. I couldn't *believe* it. I came, you know, in mid-*sentence*. It knocked me out. You know what I mean? I couldn't believe it!'

'I know exactly what you mean,' I said.

It Definitely Isn't Mohair

'Did you like fucking me?' asked Vicky later that day.

'Yes,' I said.

'Why do you say "yes" like that?'

'I couldn't very well say "no", could I?'

'But you meant "no", right?'

'No. I didn't. I meant what a daft question.'

'Don't you know premature ejaculation indicates a basic unwillingness to get involved?'

'I reckon it's got the right idea then.'

'I reckon you need help.'

'For God's sake: Marvin came in.'

'So what? You don't have to be afraid of Marvin. Marvin's gay anyway.'

'I'm not afraid of Marvin.'

'I know you're not,' said Vicky. 'I'm sorry.' She opened her large mouth in surrender and showed me her teeth. She knew I liked this. 'Listen, Connie asked us round tonight. You want to go?'

'OK.'

'You'll have to get out of those for a start.'

'Why?'

'You look like a loser.'

'You mean I look like a premature ejaculator.'

'Exactly. Ha!'

I put on my suit.

'You're not wearing THAT?' said Vicky.

'What's wrong with it?'

'The trousers are too short.'

'Are they? No they're not.'

'Is it supposed to be shiny or what?'

'Of course it's supposed to be shiny.'

'What's it made of, nylon?'

'It's mohair.'

'It definitely isn't mohair.'

I ended up in what I'd had on before.

'You'll have to be more together,' said Vicky, imagining she'd won a major victory. She picked up some of the offending garments and flung them into a cupboard in the hall. What was going on? She already had me making the breakfast and collecting her contact lenses. It was an achievement of a kind. But what kind? This was like a parody of two people setting up home together. I tried to explain.

'You know you're really full of pain,' she told me. 'Connie

agrees with me that there is really so much pain in your eyes . . .'

Of course! I had to be sick, otherwise why wasn't I in love with her?

'There you are,' said Vicky. 'You should see yourself.'

I looked in the mirror and sure enough my face was contorted with irritation.

'You should come to Group,' she said.

Later, at Connie's, she told me to sit behind her chair, not to walk about like that. When I asked why, she hissed that 'Roger never took his hands off me in public.'

'What about in private?' I asked.

'A gold medallist,' she said. 'You better believe it.'

Obviously Vicky was trying hard to persuade herself that I was a good thing. The trouble was that we were both hopelessly caricatured in one another's eyes. We kept shaking each other's image, but they remained blurred and ridiculous.

'You know something?' whispered Vicky. 'Connie says you aren't my type.'

'Connie,' I said out loud, 'what's this about my not being Vicky's type?'

'I didn't say you weren't her type,' said Connie quickly. 'I said you weren't *my* type.'

Anyone Can See You Never Rode in a Cadillac

Boston station was like a disused meat market, open on the side to driving sleet. I telephoned my host.

'Is that Mrs Hall?'

'No, this is Sue Miller,' said a firm voice. 'My husband is Ray Hall. Is that Hugo Williams? Yes, we're expecting you. Ray is at a committee meeting tonight. I thought we might go out to a meal later if I can get the child off. You've got the address? The name on the bell is James.'

I took a taxi to Berry Street.

'Number 10 seems to be a church,' said the driver. The rum-looking grey shed had 'South Boston Revivalist Chapel' written on it in red. I got his tip wrong, then couldn't open the car door.

'Anyone can see you never rode in a Cadillac before. This is the only Cadillac in the South Boston Cab Service.'

I found myself standing on a littered sidewalk, blacks slouching by me, curious or drunk, muttering. A black kid emerged. A man stood by his running motor. I went up and rang some bells. A huge black momma appeared at the top of a flight of stairs. This lady wasn't Mrs Hall surely?

'Who's you looking for, sonny?'

'Are you Mrs James?'

'No, I'se Mrs Patterson.'

'I was looking for a lady with a young child.'

'Wha's de name of de chile?'

'I don't know.'

'What street you looking for?'

'Maybe I got the wrong Berry Street.'

'This is Boston, sonny.'

'Maybe I should be in Cambridge.'

'You said it, sonny.'

I found a stinking old cab whose half crazy black driver said did I want Berry Street South Cambridge or North Cambridge. It came to me that he was asking me where it was. I asked in a garage and sure enough there was only one Berry Street in Cambridge. I found Number 10 and rang the bell marked 'James'.

Inside all was calm. The child had not gone off so I spent the first hour talking to its black doll named Nicholas about Walt Disney's *Jungle Book*. A poster of Bertolt Brecht loomed over us.

Mr Hall was still in his committee, so later his wife and I repaired to a log-cabin type cinema-restaurant complex dedicated to Orson Welles, where we searched among the bits of curry for common acquaintances and subjects fit for discourse. (Few.)

Back home, there was Ray: whiskies to drink and names of poets to knock back and forth like hot potatoes. Had I published a book myself? This was odd, I thought, as it was Ray who had invited me to read. Had he ever heard of me, I wondered. Books of poetry were passed across to me like buckets of water at a fire. A pile developed by my chair. Clayton Eshelmann, I confessed, was a poet I had never really studied. Arriving nowhere rather late, we pulled nightcaps well down over our heads and I went to bed on the dining room floor.

How Many Chairs Do You Need Exactly?

Early next morning I was offered more little ethnic dolls to inspect while Mrs Hall broke things for breakfast near by. But something was amiss. Now here was Ray standing in the doorway of the dining room with a painful expression on his face. Mumps had come on in the night. The poor man was clearly terrified. Yet he was apologising to me, and I was forgiving him. Obviously he couldn't take me to the reading, scheduled for the afternoon, or introduce me. Mrs Hall would have to do it. You know, honey, the large tower near the road. You take the elevator in back of the refectory. As it turned out, she didn't know at all.

A garrison of the New Brutalism, stuck on a wind-raked peninsula of Massachusetts Bay. Miniature students, blown inside out by the rain-soaked wind, seemed to accentuate the desolation. Wavelets rippled across the vast puddles which had settled on the pedestrian precincts. Some students battled past in wheelchairs. No doubt the architects thought of them when they ignored the rest of humanity. The wind moaned through a beastly tunnel connecting two quads. We took the lift to the office. No one had heard of us. For whom were we looking exactly? Mrs Hall was uncertain where we were expected. We stumbled on the refectory and sat down to prune yoghurt and stuffed turkey. After further enquiries, we found our way to an obscure venue called 'The English Lounge'. This was empty, except for an agreeable-looking blonde girl who said she wasn't stopping for the reading, but could I sign here for the money, which they couldn't let me have unfortunately, as they had to send it to England later, after tax of course.

About eight people drifted in, then three more, then Mrs Hall said as there was no one to introduce me I'd better begin. I'd just got started when a fat girl came in saying we weren't to mind her, she only wanted to make coffee. She made her way to the kitchenette at the back of the room, put on the kettle and stood there staring at me until it boiled. She made herself a cup, smiled at the ceiling and wandered away with it through the door. I didn't mind when this happened a second time, but when two massive black men came in and started counting the empty chairs I had to stop and find out what was going on. 'How many chairs do you need exactly?' one of them asked me.

'Only the ones being used.' ''Cos we need them for the political meeting.' At first I thought he wanted all of them. 'How many do you want?' 'Only twenty-six.' And they proceeded to air-lift every free chair out of the door.

'Do you consider yourself to be a craftsman?' someone asked when the reading was over.

'A craftsman?'

'Do you spend a long time on each poem?'

'Yes, but it's more like gambling than carpentry. You keep thinking you're just about to hit on the winning system, the right system of mistakes. You're betting on yourself, but the reader has to keep up with the horse – or very nearly. That's what makes the betting so difficult. Each time you say to yourself, just one more bet . . .'

'I understand,' said the questioner.

Another man, a teacher, said he was delighted someone was attempting the long poem. In the confusion over the chairs, I'd forgotten to read out the titles of my poems. Titles sound pompous-daft read out loud anyway. This man hadn't noticed. He thought I'd managed the long form magnificently. He wanted to congratulate me on the overall grandeur of my theme. He wouldn't say what this was exactly, despite my pumping him, but he did say he thought it was all rock solid. Fine.

I left the stand and looked around for Mrs Hall to guide me from the labyrinth. We approached each other across the room, our mouths open ready to reply to what the other was about to say. Neither of us spoke. I held the door open for her and she passed under my arm without a word. We picked our way among the puddles of the campus, through a cindery car park and up over a bridge to the subway. Here we contemplated an advertisement for A. E. Long's Funeral Homes. 'Service is a Long Word' it said, until the train arrived, swallowing our silence.

The Need to Get Hostel

'Where *have* you been?' said Vicky when I got back. 'I wanted you to meet Dean. He came all the way from Dallas just to check me out.'

'What happened?'

'Nothing. Absolutely nothing. I failed. I was uptight. I don't know why. I wasn't open. He went back to Dallas already.'

'So. You didn't hit it off.'

'Hit it off! Hit it off! He came all the way from Dallas just to check out my head. He said I'd changed. He was right. He left his manuscript. You can read it if you like.'

I picked up the grubby ream:

> Ghosts of rock-hard lavender tubes were late
> For the island trainer whose washing line
> Overshot its own pretty threshold ban sometimes.

'It's the usual New York tripe,' I said.

'Dean is serious about his work,' said Vicky.

'He sounds a creep.'

'He was honest with me.'

'You didn't fancy him, so he put you down.'

'Sex is more than just fancying someone, you know.'

'More like fancying someone you don't know perhaps?'

'You English you're so fucked up. You're dishonest with yourselves. No wonder you're so fucked up.'

'We're not fucked up, we're just exhausted.'

'You're so uptight. You should go see Louie. He'd soon straighten your head for you.'

'Who's Louie now?'

'Louie's a shrink if you want to know. One of the best.'

'I'm shrink-resistant.'

'You're basically dishonest.'

'Pay some smoothie to listen to my life? Then he puts it in his novel. No thanks. Maybe he's one of these ones you shout at. That I'd like.'

'Ah. Hostel. No need to get hostel. Boy, have you got prab-lems!'

'I was in a good mood a minute ago. I think I'll get some sleep.'

'You can't go in there. Marvin's in there with Sean. You better take the day-bed.'

Vicky Tires of New York

Soon after this I took to staying out at night whenever possible, coming back to sleep in my/Marvin's room when he was out.

One morning he and Vicky were having extremely casual sex in 'my' bed when I got back there after one of these nights. I made for the couch.

'Don't go,' said Vicky, 'I want to talk to you about something.'

'Yes, but . . .' It was obvious that Marvin found my presence counter-romantic.

'Marvin doesn't mind, do you Marv?'

'N-no,' said Marvin, his face at painful cross-purposes with itself as he tried to smile hello. You could see he wanted to stop doing what he was doing, but he seemed to have no choice. Vicky, on top of him, was perfectly at ease.

'I'm sick of New York,' she announced, gazing moodily out across Bleecker Street.

'So am I,' I said, longing for bed.

'Health freaks!' said Vicky. 'It's so goddam depressing. A frosty fag-town, Dean Moriarty called it . . .'

Marvin glanced at me for help. I shrugged my shoulders.

'I tell you what I wanted to ask you,' said Vicky. 'I thought maybe you knew a place I could stay in London . . . maybe your place? All I need is a bed and phone, you know what I mean?' She put on her most appealing face.

'Do you know Jimmy and Rose Wexler?' I suggested, starting to enjoy the show.

'I don't think so,' said Vicky, furrowing her brow. 'Are they Americans?'

There was a look of deep shock on Marvin's face by now.

'I'll write down a few names for you,' I said as I went out. 'Do you want some tea?'

'Thanks,' moaned Marvin.

Solomon's Gay Pride Button

'You looked so embarrassed walking in on us like that,' said Vicky later.

'I was only pretending to be,' I said.

'How come?'

'I wanted to laugh.'

'Why didn't you then?'

'I suppose you were trying to shock me?'

'As a matter of fact . . . I can't remember.'

178

'What about poor old Marvin though?'

'Marvin talks too much. I had to go to bed with him just to stop him talking . . .'

'I don't think I've ever heard him speak.'

'Sex makes you feel awkward, doesn't it?'

'Not in the least.'

'I believe you're jealous of Marvin.'

'No I'm not.'

'I can see it in your eyes.'

'No you can't.'

'You know what you should do? You should come to Group with me some time.'

'No-no.'

'I feel sure you'd just grow tremendously from it.'

'Not me.'

'I took Solomon one time, as well as Tarquin and David Bukofski. You remember Solomon? With the gay pride button? He broke down completely. It was incredible.'

'In what sense?'

'He confessed to this entire room full of strangers that he'd always hated his father and that he'd never made love to anyone in his life.'

'Were these two things thought to be connected in some way?'

'Naturally!'

'Naturally? You mean he hated his father because he couldn't find a girlfriend?'

'No. He couldn't find a girlfriend because he hated his father . . . I mean . . .'

'Look, if I was a girl I wouldn't fancy Solomon anyway.'

'You're so ignorant, Hugo, you know that? You're full of . . .'

'Ignorance?'

'Louie said it was one of the most beautiful things he's ever seen.'

'What was?'

'Solomon breaking down like that.'

You Must Be Canadian, Right?

'My life's falling apart,' said the man sitting next to me at the Connaught Bar. I looked round and saw a small, beaky man staring into a large drink. A little dog with hopeless, popping eyes sat next to the drink, staring at me.

'I said my life's falling apart,' said the little man again, in some irritation.

'No it isn't,' I said, already regretting it.

'Come again?' said the little man, looking round in surprise.

'No it isn't.'

'Tell me something,' said the little man. 'What you know about my life anyway?'

'Nothing. Have a peanut.'

'How do you like this guy!' said the man, looking round for support. 'I tell him my life's falling apart, he tells me I'm wrong. How do you like this guy?'

'Calm down, Harry,' said the girl on his right. 'You're not to mind Harry. He gets upset sometimes, don't you Harry? You a friend of Harry's or something? Harry needs a nice friend like you . . .'

A slightly pissed blonde wearing a miniature top hat was approaching me.

'I've never seen him before,' I said.

'Never seen him before? Never seen Harry? You must be Canadian, right?'

'English.'

'English? Oh, English! Right! Hey, you gotta meet Shelley. Shelley went to Europe one time . . . Hey, Shelley . . . meet English . . .' She went back to Harry and Shelley took over. Shelley had legs up to the sky and a tiny face like a daisy. A menthol ad in Lurex. She put her arm round my neck and had some of my drink. I bought her one of her own and she threw it back. In a cloud of cosmetic power she said I was the best-in-the-world and pinched my bottom. I bought her another drink and she said she was in love with Tim Curry. She said the *Rocky Horror Picture Show* was the best-in-the-world. I put my arm round her waist and she said I must write to her when I got back to England, and did I know someone called Anwat Singh who worked in Debenham's. I said I'd write to her right now if she liked, but she said no, she was staying with her mom right now.

It must have been then that I saw Omar. He came over and we went outside for a smoke. When I tried to get back into the Connaught with my drink, the doorman blocked my way.

'You wanna get me arrested?' he snarled. 'I know what you've been up to. Put your glass down there and don't try to show your face in here again, y'unnerstan?'

Shelley was just coming out with the small man and the girl in the miniature top hat and Omar said we could all go to Birdland. He had free passes for the opening.

Captain of Starship Atari

In Omar's car the small man had to sit on my lap. His career was in ruins, he told everyone. He'd been offered the part of the Tin Soldier in *Hans Andersen*, only to be told they'd decided to animate his section. I thought this was a refreshing sort of story for New York and I laughed a little bit. His pop-eyed dog licked my face in sympathy.

'What's so funny?' asked the small man. 'My wife left me. I'm on welfare. I'm four foot eight. They repossessed my car . . .'

Birdland was the top floor of a skyscraper on Wall Street. We went up in the lift, the doors opened and there was this dazzling dance floor spreading into the distance with the lights of New York for backdrop. Acres of naked male torsos shimmied enthusiastically on every hand and not a few naked male buttocks to boot. The bar-boys wore jock-straps. A naked black man go-go'd frantically on a shelf. Sweat flew. Only the three kneeling models on diamanté leashes held by a man in an executioner's mask looked remotely cool.

Shelley wouldn't dance, so I bounced round on my own for a while. The place was really a gymnasium and it had a sprung floor. I got as far as the bar and there was Shelley and the top hat waiting for me. The round cost $20. I was just finding out that the top hat was an avant-garde conjuror's assistant called Sue, when a gay jumped on the bar with a padlock through his foreskin. There was a chain through the padlock with something edible attached to it which you were supposed to try and nibble. This appealed to Sue's professional side and she ran around trying to find out the man's name. She said she was very excited about making her act with Cicero more erotic. She seemed brittle and half-baked, but brassy enough. I listened to her plans for a while, then she opened her eyes very wide as if she had just seen me.

'Do you dislike me?' she asked perceptively.

'Not at all.'

'Do you know many gays?' – narrowing her eyes as if she had spotted the missing ingredient in my life.

'Yes, lots.'

'Aren't they outrageous?'

'Outrageous?' So that's what they were!

'I spend all my time with gays.'

'Why is that?'

'I'm waiting for David.'

'David who?'

'David Bowie of course.'

'You're waiting for David Bowie?'

'Let's put it this way. I figure if I go to all the places David might go to for six months, and I never get to meet him during all that time, then I'll accept that I'm not supposed to meet him.' She pushed some money into a tele-game and started jumping up and down.

'And you think he might come to a place like this?'

'Anthea saw him at The Pyramids one time . . .'

'I know, but . . .'

Sue's un-dead personality was closing in on me. I'd started the evening sharp as paint. Now I was an old man in a dry month. Many years ago I had been able to take an interest in my surroundings, make jokes, laugh. Now I could hardly cope with my cigarette.

'Which of David's albums do you like best?' asked Sue.

'*Hunky Dory.*'

'I never liked that one so much. I don't think David likes that one himself any more . . .'

'SCORE 3000,' announced Sue's tele-game, 'CRASHES 3. DE-POSIT 25C TO BECOME CAPTAIN OF STARSHIP ATARI!!!'

Two girls had started dancing in a spotlight below the shelf where the naked black man was revolving his stomach. I noticed a thin jet of water cascading down on to them. I looked up and saw that the man was peeing on the girls. Everyone was clapping like mad. An expression of satisfied delight spread over Sue's six-year-old's face. She clapped her hands excitedly, saying:

'Isn't he outrageous?'

'He's the best in the world,' I said.

I suddenly wanted to pee myself, but foresaw a problem. The gents seemed to be a feature of Birdland. In fact, most people were more interested in the gents than the bar. It jutted on to the dance-floor like a piece of stage scenery. It had bulbs outlining it and the euphemism 'GENTS' went on and off in blue and red. I put my head round the door and saw what looked like a failed cocktail party in progress — lots of ominous-looking men hanging aroung waiting to be introduced, but no host. If they can't reproduce, how come there's always more of them?

'Good Bowie-hunting,' I said to Sue, 'I'm leaving now.'

I went down in the lift and rejoined the freezing, realistic night. Deep beneath the skyscraper, the grim subway was the other side of the coin. The deafening trains with their spray-gun graffiti looked like dingy Chinese dragons the day after a festival. An 'E' train hurtled by, turning the station inside out like a sock. 'IT'S TIME TO TURN YOUR SKIN TO SILK WITH SOLUTION OF ARABIA.' Little human figures, barely sketched in against the massive pillars and echoing perspectives, scurried for their burrows like thieves, the big bundles of tomorrow's *New York Sunday Times* tucked under their arms like swag. An old man ran by, holding something to his eye.

An Abundance of Thick, Creamy Bubbles

I got back to Vicky's house, then changed my mind about going inside. Marvin was bound to be in the bed, possibly with Vicky. I got out my address book and phoned everyone I knew in New York. The first person to answer was Paula, the vacillating Japanese print importer. I didn't say anything, but walked to her hotel and used the house phone to prepare her for my strange arrival. She seemed pleased enough to hear my voice until she understood that I was presently downstairs and keen to come instantly on up. She tried to get out of it, but I said I *had* to see her and finally she relented. But only for a minute, she said. Naturally, she was expecting a call.

The elevator wouldn't come, so I bounded drunkenly up the stairs, for once in my life experiencing the joy of positive action, however spurious. The door opened and Paula's silk-wrapped body flopped into my arms, her skin deliciously hot still from the bed, which we fell back into.

Out bodies were soon twisted into a single rope, but it wasn't long before I realised that all I wanted to do at that moment was pee. I disentwined myself from Paula's arms and made for the bathroom. When I got there I found I couldn't go. I hummed a tune. I dimmed the lights. I put all the taps on. In vain my puerile senses went sashaying along the rows of unfamiliar skin creams and bath salts. 'Fill your tub with an abundance of thick, creamy bubbles,' I read. 'Being pH balanced, Village Bubble Bath will maintain your skin's natural acid mantle.' 'Mambo Talcum – the powder with the Latin American tang.' I was half way through the small print on a bottle of green fluid – (did she straighten her hair, or what?) – when it suddenly occurred to me that I had been standing in this girl's bathroom for more than five minutes. It was horrible. Why on earth didn't I go while I was downstairs? I could have sobered up, had a wash. Everything would have been fine. Now it was the end of the world. Paula was probably lying in bed listening, waiting for me. Obviously she could hear everything I was doing, or not doing, even if I couldn't hear her. She must be wondering how much longer I was going to be. Perhaps she wanted to go herself? No, no, for God's sake keep that thought back or we'll be here for ever.

I pushed my pants and trousers right down to my ankles to get more freedom. I stood there listening to my brain apologising to me. I had long ago abandoned the counting method, which consists of counting in tens, if sober enough, or, if not, of muttering hundreds of ludicrously random figures until a breakthrough is achieved by a process of alienation. One of these always works. Not this time.

I arranged for redskins to do a war-dance roung the rim of a tea-cup. I had milk-bottles water-skiing, dock leaves doing push-ups. Something like recognition flickered faintly between my legs, then numbness returned to the world.

Suddenly I was back in the makeshift gents behind the tote at a point-to-point long ago. My father had queued with me for twenty minutes to get as far as the tent-flaps. Now we were inside. I took one look at the stained canvas pouches you were supposed to pee into and got the first refusal from my independently minded bladder. 'Do it on the ground,' said my father, seeing I was too short to reach the shocking receptacle. 'I can't,' I said. 'Christ!' said my father. He picked me up and held me in front of the thing for a minute. This was worse than useless and I started crying. In the end we had to go to the ladies, which was more like home, and I was all right.

But I was in a ladies now! What was the matter with me?

'Do it on the ground,' I heard my father saying. 'I can't,' I said out loud.

For something to do I opened the medicine cabinet and saw row upon row of pill boxes and medicine bottles, a sight I usually find irresistible. For God's sake don't touch, I thought, or the whole lot is going to fall out and you'll be back to square one. I moved a large bottle slightly to see if it was really full of Quaaludes. Another one, balanced on top of it, fell down and broke in the lavatory. Red and blue capsules stared up at me from the bottom of a well. Where was I? Not still in this bloody bathroom? I put out a hand to steady myself and let out a cry as I burnt myself on the towel rail.

I wondered again what Paula must be thinking. Had I burst upon the scene so impetuously only to lock myself in her lavatory for the night? Was I some kind of closet person? Was I dangerous perhaps? If only I could know she'd given up and gone back to sleep I'd be all right. I decided to give it one more go. I took off my shoes, to get a firmer balance on the deep pile carpet. I took my trousers off completely. I leant my forehead on the cupboard and told myself that it was all over now anyway, so I might as well give up. I imagined Paula ringing for the porters to come and break down the door and take me away. I realised that any minute now I'd have to go back in there with my hands up. I told myself that maybe if I lay down it wouldn't hurt so much.

There was a knock on the door:

'Are you all right in there?'

'Sure,' I said, pulling the chain in an everyday sort of way.

There's Nothing Wrong with the Bathroom, It's You

I emerged from the bathroom sober.

'I have to tell you something,' I said, 'I think there's something the matter with your bathroom. It has a strange effect on me . . .'

'You must be *crazy*. There's nothing wrong with my bathroom. It's you. You're drunk.'

'Look, I have to go downstairs for a moment. I won't be a second. You hang on here.'

'GO DOWNSTAIRS? You're out of your mind! It's FOUR IN THE MORNING!'

I had been standing in the beautiful, empty, silent gents of the Hilton Bar for two whole minutes before it dawned on me: I didn't want to go! I hadn't wanted to go all along! That was the reason I hadn't been able to go in Paula's bathroom: there was nothing to go with. Why didn't I think of that? The problem was, what *did* I want to do? I thought of Paula's hot, silk-wrapped body, full of passionate sleepiness and I knew what I wanted to do. I got on the house-phone. Paula answered, then hung up. OK. I took the lift. I knocked. Paula's voice sounded loud:

'You're WEIRD!' she said. 'FUCK OFF!'

'You know what my mother used to say?' said the man behind the bar in the Hilton all-night coffee shop, carrying on the conversation he'd been having with his previous customer.

'No,' I said, 'what did she used to say?'

' "Never misbehave," she used to tell me. She used that word, "misbehave", she didn't say "screw" or "fuck", she used to call it "misbehavin' ". "Never misbehave," she used to say, "except with a girl you wouldn't be ashamed to marry afterwards." '

'Marry?' I said.

'You know what she used to tell me?' He looked me straight in the eye. 'She used to say "One pubic hair on a woman is more powerful than a herd of wild horses." That's what she used to say. And she meant it literally. She didn't fuck around, my old mother.'

Straight On Till Morning

It's broad daylight. Your feet ache and you're not looking good any more. It's time to go home and get some sleep. You think, 'Just one more street, then I'll be sensible.' You get to the end of the street and it seems like a more attractive idea to carry on to the next one. Another street, another drink, another bet, it's the same feeling of diminished responsibility for the ultimate outcome of your choice, of surrender to the gorgeous dog-ends of circumstance.

186

It's easy to feel like that in New York when you first get there. You're like 'The Mummy'. You have that look in your eye that says, 'For God's sake don't stop me now.' You stay up all night and don't have a hangover. You fall in love with the strange plumes of steam that linger on every street corner. You start talking faster. You decide to move to New York for good and everyone you meet finds this quite natural.

Then suddenly it's over. You wake one morning and you feel like your old self again. You buy a newspaper or something. You think it's going to rain. Then New York will never be the same for you again and the next person you ring up is surprised to hear you're still around and seems to be wondering what there could be to warrant a second — or was it a third? — meeting between you. Do you have a project in mind, or what?

Turning Up My Collar in Central Park

It was ten in the morning when I saw Central Park glittering ahead of me. There were clouds of blossom at their four-day peak and I felt happy to be walking about like that with nowhere to go and nothing boring to attend to on that spring morning. I felt experienced and a little drunk still, breathing the crisp air.

I wrapped my jacket tighter and pushed my hands down deeper into my pockets, smiling tolerantly at my stupid joy in the world. For a rare moment I was convinced of the rightness of my own casting in it. There I was! Didn't I fit the part like a glove? I felt pleased by my own familiar weight which I could move forward so effortlessly. I liked the feel of the cold wind blowing through my suit.

I watched the frisbee throwers gyrating like Matisse cut-outs on either side of an arena. The orange frisbee flew in a smooth arc against the distant shell of the concert platform — to be caught or missed or knocked into the air with the knuckles, once, twice, three times, before being caught and flung back with a fluid baseball backhand. Now and then it would hit the ground, skitter a moment, then take off again, wobbling now, to be caught low down on the run. One boy trapped it with his foot and a shout rang out, 'Anything you do to that frisbee I'm gonna do to you two times.'

There was a lake near by and the rocks in the middle were

smeared with graffiti. Someone must have swum out with a magic-marker in his pocket: 'Killer', 'Sex 7', 'So Wild Inc.', 'Tracy'. The day-glo colours mocked the phoney pastoral setting. The balustrades and pillars of the parade where I was sitting were likewise faithfully disfigured: 'Bowie', 'Fu-Fu', 'Whitee of 101st St', 'Hunter Claws 120th', their names for themselves entering the battle with time alongside the busts of Schiller and Beethoven, looking composed on their plinths. A half-tame squirrel approached me in a series of doubtful side-tracks. He stood up and looked at me in amazement before being called away by a friend. A horse carriage suddenly swept by with some Indians on board, their blue and pink saris afloat in the breeze. Then the whole of New York was like a piece of floating blue smoke blown momentarily across my sight as I stood there screwing up my eyes in the sun. I realised that this was a fictional world I was in, a world in which I had no part to play and therefore no existence to hinder my happiness. But on that pristine morning in Central Park I felt as if I could triumph over any madness that might be waiting for me beyond the trees, and I turned up my collar to disguise my secret delight in the world.

I Feel As If I'm Falling Out the Window

I'd strained my back moving Vicky's desk into the hall. When she asked me to move it back into the living room, I refused. Vicky stood there, mustering her reserves.

'It's sexual tension,' she said. 'That's all it is. You accept your body, you release all that confusion into the atmosphere. You become *strong*.'

'I DO accept my body. It's weak and I accept that.'

'No you don't. You reject it. Look at the way you sit – all slumped down. Stand up! Like this!'

Living with Vicky was a nerve-racking process. It was like performing some weird modern satire. One morning I tried to pull down the blind alongside the bed on which we were trying unsuccessfully to make love in full view of all the people going to work down Bleecker Street.

'What you do that for?' asked Vicky, breaking off her discourse on the films of Jean Renoir.

'I feel as if I'm falling out the window,' I said.

'You're so uptight. Just relax, can't you?' And she let the blind go up again. 'Ricardo used to make love to me in Central Park.'

The trouble with Vicky was that she wanted to dominate everything in the world except the last moment of lovemaking, which she expected to carry all before it in a gorgeous swoon. And the trouble with me was that I found it impossible to grab the reins that late in the proceedings.

'Impotence is the denial of pleasure through guilt,' she told me.

'Last week it was bad toilet training.'

'That too is a possibility. By the way, it's your turn to do out the john . . .'

'I'm definitely not doing out the john.'

Looking back, I still get caught in the web of self-contradictions, boasts and delusions of splendour that made up Vicky's retirement from the world. I think of her yanked mouth and the ghastly boredom of her harangues, a shrink-induced separateness which she shared with half the female population of this city.

'You're full of pain,' she said, when I told her I was moving out into a boarding house for my last two weeks. 'You see yourself as a second class citizen, therefore a traveller. You're so full of pain it's pathetic.'

That was before I became 'full of anger' and, finally, 'full of shit'.

10

GOODBYE NEW YORK

The Guest List

Dr Feelgood's manager is a big person with a soft spot for all forms of physical excess. He has fists like old car crashes. His knees are urban disaster areas. He is the kind of person who might under other circumstances have worn a brown pinstripe or been tattooed with mermaids, but who today wears a black T-shirt and dark glasses and manages a rock band.

Chris was in town with the idea of getting to know the place intimately in the forty hours available to him and with the aid of whatever people or things that happened to present themselves. The first thing he had to do, he said, was to see the big comeback concert of an American group called Group B. They weren't any good, he said, but there was a party afterwards we could go to. I went to his hotel and we started to get into training for the occasion. By the time the limousine arrived we were as fit as fleas.

Chris sat in the front and talked to the driver about the Korean war. I sat in the back with the PR officer and her staff, whose jobs were on the line that night. I was feeling car-sick, but the PR wouldn't have the window down because of her hair.

'What band is it again?' I asked, trying to take my mind off the rolling motion of the limousine.

'What BAND is it?' said the PR in horror. 'What are you doing here if you don't know what BAND it is?'

'I'm with him,' I said, pointing to Chris.

'It's Group B,' said the PR. 'And you're lucky to get in.'

'Are they any good these days?' I asked.

'Of course they're any good,' said the PR, 'otherwise I wouldn't be working for them, would I?'

'Wouldn't you?'

'No I wouldn't.'

'I was just trying to make you feel it wouldn't be your fault if they bombed again,' I said, winding down the window.

'They're not going to BOMB!'

'Are they disco nowadays? Or do they call it soul?'

'They're r 'n b.'

'They definitely aren't r 'n b.'

'Who IS this?' asked the PR, winding up the window. 'Who put him in the limousine?'

'I did,' said Chris, turning round and charming her. Chris thinks I am a gentleman of leisure, who should, by rights, always travel in limousines. 'He's our biographer,' he said.

'The Guest List is supposed to be Company only,' said the PR. 'I'm going to have a word with Mr Trotter about this.'

I wound the window down again and breathed hard for a moment.

'If you're so against the B's,' said the PR, 'What are you going to their concert for?'

She had a point.

'We're going to the party afterwards, aren't we?' I said, looking at Chris.

'We'll see about that,' said the PR, furiously winding up the window again.

The Backstage Pass

Group B were worse than anyone had expected. I was sitting apart from Chris and I accidentally fell asleep, despite the racket. A Group B fan sitting next to me jogged me awake without a smile, then changed places with her boyfriend, who didn't pass on any of the joints that were mugging me with their aromas.

Afterwards, the PR came up to me and said triumphantly that Chris had already gone backstage, so I was on my own.

'I'll go round later,' I said.

'Not without a backstage pass you won't.'

Chris had just given me his own pass, but I didn't let on.

'Don't worry,' I said. 'I'll slip through somehow. Weren't they terrible?' I stuck my finger in my ear. 'I've got tinnitus!'

'They're a smash,' said the PR.

The Pick-Me-Up

'Cosmo, you've done it again man,' a fan was saying when I got to the backstage bar.

'You reckon?' said the guitarist moodily.

'You better believe it, man. You were rocking out. You blew me away.'

'Yeah?'

'Like, how did you rate the gig yourself? You looked really . . .'

'You know in *Boncecraft*? Where I hide behind the speaker?'

'Yeah.'

'I couldn't see Jim at all. Was he with us or what?'

'Jim? Don't you mean Greg, man?'

'Greg? On bass?'

'No, Kevin plays bass nowadays. Doesn't he?'

'I thought there were supposed to be five of us on stage . . .'

'Not since El Paso, surely?'

'El Paso . . .' said the guitarist slowly. 'Where are we now then?'

I tried to get to the bar, but it was impossible. Then I tried to get away from the bar. I saw the PR drinking out of a whisky bottle. Chris appeared.

'We're going to the opening of some new niterie,' he said. 'You wanna go?'

'Love to.'

'You look a little bit peaky still. You need a pick-me-up.'

We went into the nearest toilet and got out the pick-me-up, which worked wonders. I fought my way to the bar and started talking to a singer called Sandwich about Andrew Loog Old-ham. Sandwich had a piercing crazy look and wouldn't stay still for a second. Pinocchio face . . . high heels . . . carroty hair . . . bell-bottomed jeans . . . red comb . . . My head started to spin and I asked Sandwich to get me a glass of water. I had to sit down. I hung my head and instantly a thin black woman sat down next to me and offered me a joint. She was a

Virgo, she said, with something else rising. She shook her head and showed me a pendant with a scarab beetle on it given to her by 'Jim Morrison'. I tried to look at the beetle, but felt sick and had to look down again.

'*You* know,' she said. 'Jim Morrison of the Doors.'

'Yes,' I said, 'I know who you mean, dead, right?'

'Aren't you American then?'

'Of course I'm American.'

Unwisely, I took some of the joint. I was soon panting for oxygen. I felt simultaneously restless and weak. I made the usual mistake of seeking fresh air. I got as far as the corridor and collapsed on some woman's back.

The world came slowly back into being with sparkling fogs giving way to faces saying things about water, air and blood.

'The person from Dr Feelgood has fainted,' said someone.

'He looks pretty sick. Did he hit his head?'

'No, I didn't,' I said, trying to sit up. 'I'm fine now.' I didn't want the PR to see me lying on the floor like that. I must have passed out again, because the next thing I knew there was an ugly suntanned old woman sitting next to me in the lotus position telling me about her career as a dancer in pre-revolutionary Cuba. She took hold of my head and said she was going to re-balance it correctly on my atlas vertebra.

'How old do you think I am?' she asked.

'Sixty?'

'I'm sixty-three.'

'What are you doing on the floor?' said Chris, appearing at last out of the crowd.

'I passed out.'

'You better get up. We're going to this club.'

'I don't think he should,' said the old woman. 'The blood-sugar loss to the brain . . .'

'A glass of tequila,' said Chris. 'That's what he needs.'

The tequila was added to my collection of cures. That and the post-fainting adrenalin soon had me back on my feet and feeling thrilled with everything once more.

'Come aboard the Pepsi Generation!' said Dave Johannsen comfortingly as we walked through the fabulous New York midnight to his car. 'The Youthquake! Christ Almighty!'

Dave's retinue had been snowballing all evening with people like me. Now there were so many people in his car he was having difficulty steering. We visited a number of out-of-the-way clubs with David always gallantly going in last to make sure we all got in. When we got to the Black Dice, half the concert audience was there tucking into free food.

'Not another queer club?' said Chris, surveying the frantic bustle.

'I don't think so,' I said.

'What do you mean by queer exactly?' asked a man with a little dog in a special pocket stitched to his shoulder.

'What indeed?' said Chris.

Group B's pert PR was slumped at a table near the door, her rinsed hair spread out in front of her with several glasses and a handbag on it. This put me in a good mood and I had a dance on my own, which seemed to be all right.

'Do you know what Paul Morrissey has just said?' said someone from the car, running up to me in a panic.

'No, what?'

'He said, "The people here look as though they've mugged black people and are wearing their clothes," isn't it incredible?'

'Incredible.'

'And so true, don't you think?'

'Not really.'

'Are you British then?'

'Yes.'

'That why you dress like the sixties or are those just your clothes?'

'They're just my clothes.'

We stood in silence for a moment, watching a contortionist stir her cocktail with her toe. No one else seemed to care about her. Suddenly she got up and flounced out of the room.

My God! Vicky! I saw her teeth flashing on the far side of the club and made my way over there. I bought her a drink and we stood watching a boxing match on video and arguing about her latest therapy: crotch-eyeballing. 'Ever try mooning?' I asked. I knew she was being contrary for my benefit, and I pretended to be pleased when she said I was a Philistine. Communication, I remembered, was the problem to the answer with Vicky. We had a cross little dance and I said:

'Whatever else I may have said to you, I say to you now that you've got guts, you've really got guts.' I was pretty drunk by now.

'Of course I have, Sweetheart,' said Vicky, kissing me triumphantly. Then she was gone.

'On course for oblivion, Captain?' said Chris in passing.

'On course, Captain.'

'Psst,' said the next person from somewhere behind me. I turned round and came face to face with a big old girl buckled tightly into Hell's Angel gear. There was some dried blood on her sleeve.

'Psst,' she said, looking through me.

'Psst or pissed?'

'Let me tell you a thing,' said the girl, mimicking male bonhomie. 'I was in Vietnam, you know. I fought for my country. Gave the best years of my life. Now look at me . . .'

I looked at her and she didn't look so bad.

'You didn't actually fight, did you?'

'Sure I did. I was top-paid markswoman. A sniper. Annie Oakley. Spot on! Now I work at Spartacus. How d'ya like that?' She handed me a card. Obviously she didn't like it:

SPARTACUS ROMAN BATHS
Feeling tense and uptight? Magnificently
provocative hand-maidens will minister to
your every whim. Here, in the heart of New
York's smart East Side you will find everything
you ever dreamed of and more. Complete wardrobe
for TV, enema sessions, B & D, French Culture,
Water Sports.

This hand-maiden wasn't provocative. She just wanted to talk. She squeezed my balls and I pushed her away from me, spilling our drinks. Now here was her boyfriend, utterly drunk, who wanted urgently to confide in me personally about her. This seeming beautiful girl, he explained, had 'many thoughts' inside her head, so I wasn't to take anything she said 'on face value'. One of her 'many thoughts' was clearly to shake this

195

doglike being, but it wasn't so easily achieved, as he had now become my friend as well.

'Come and see us at the club,' said the girl. 'I'll buy you a drink.'

'I can't,' I said. 'I'm going back to England tomorrow.'

The Street Lamp Fills the Gutter with Gold

It was two or three in the morning and I felt like a breath of air. The street was deserted. Plumes of moody mist stood about like silent spear-carriers. Others billowed from outlets in the side-walk. I remembered seeing these plumes of steam in the film of *Guys and Dolls* and thinking how unconvincing they were. But New York is like that. It's THE LOOK. It's so theatrical you can't believe it. You blink once in this electric city and you see the negative of the postcard, the after-image of civilisation. Teeming dark cliffs engulfed me. One skyscraper was like a ruined Mexican pyramid, its soft outline haloed by the moon. The sky was reddish velvet. The distant sound of engines was sucked upwards to be lost in a million windows. The light from high-up street lamps filtered downwards like weak snow, melting and vanishing in the oily puddles of sodden off-cuts and bits of artificial fur. An occasional stick of neon shivered in the musty dawn. 'Free Jokes and Fun Enter Here,' said a darkened bank. I stood there like Neil Armstrong on the surface of the moon, unable to take a single step for myself, let alone mankind.

Who's a Pretty Boy?

A few hours later I woke on the floor of someone's bathroom.

'Are you in there, Huge?' It sounded like Chris.

'I think so. Where am I?'

'I don't know, but we're being kicked out.'

'Where are we going now?'

'Coney Island.'

'On no, I can't.'

'Course you can. I'll get the limmo. We'll take some sup-plies.'

As it happened, Chris couldn't get the limousine. Group B were using it. We took the train to Coney Island. Every jolt was like a tiny hangover all of its own and the thought of all the fun waiting for us at the other end made me want to cry. Leaving the station by the subway, we saw the word PRAY scrawled on a wall in giant day-glo.

'We've got to see a freakshow,' said Chris good-naturedly. 'A two-headed donkey or something, knock this hangover on the head.'

'No one's knocking my hangover on the head,' I said.

'I saw a feathered woman once,' said Chris. 'She sat on a perch flapping her wings and going "Who's a pretty boy? Who's a pretty boy?" You've got to feel better after something like that.'

I could hardly have felt worse. Breakfast was out of the question and I hadn't shaved for two days. The lining of my leather jacket hung down at the back like an old shirt. Some time the previous night I'd been sick up the sleeve, which was now detaching itself from the shoulder. I took off the wretched garment and stuffed it into a trashcan marked KEEP AMERICA BEAUTIFUL.

Most of the rides were boarded up for the off-season, but one called The Cyclone reared its dragon head above the rest and blew gratuitous sparks into nothingness. The centre of activity was a mini roller-coaster called the rock 'n roller, which had a mad DJ of about sixteen who played all the latest rhythms at top volume. He went on the machine himself, standing up all the way round, doing acrobatics and allowing his friends to do the same. Their girlfriends stood round the edge, dancing and clapping them to their deaths. Shirking this unstable area, Chris and I toured the agreeably drab fairground in search of the elusive freakshow. Once we came to a hoarding which said.

See The Famous Diving Horse
Plunge Into A Barrel Of Pitch
Also Aquatic Thrills From
The Collegiate Swimmers

Chris got quite excited about this suicidal horse, but luckily it was closed for alterations. MEET THE MOVIE STARS was open however, and we took in the original bat-cycle, Jean Harlow's Jaguar, the Roadster from *Bonnie and Clyde*, the authentic guillo-

tine from *A Tale of Two Cities* and a lifesize model of Marilyn
Monroe in the nude.

After that I bought a whip, a tie and a flag and Chris bought
a pair of Hypno-Spex – each lens of which was a printed spiral
with a hole in it:

HOW TO HYPNOTISE PEOPLE WITH HYPNO-SPEX
1 Put on HYPNO-SPEX
2 Request subject to gaze into your eyes
3 Move you face to within six inches of subject's face
4 Slowly withdraw to a distance of three feet
5 Move in again
REPEAT THIS PROCESS MORE AND MORE QUICKLY UNTIL SUBJECT
FALLS INTO A DAZED CONDITION

Chris was delighted with this gadget and said he was going to
use it for negotiating Dr Feelgood's contract with the managing
director of United Artists. I was beginning to think we had
escaped having to go to the freakshow when we came to something called The Hell Hole – an imposing frontage painted
with all manner of monsters.

'This is more like it,' said Chris, and in we went. Paying our
50c to a black child of six got us through a turnstile, down a
passage and through a door into a circular chamber with an
upper gallery. A few children were hanging about waiting near
the walls.

'What the fuck's this?' said Chris.

'The Wall of Death,' I said glumly, as the place started to
revolve.

'Not the Wall of Death?' said Chris.

'I'm afraid so.'

At first it wasn't too bad – a pleasant merry-go-round effect.
But as the walls gathered speed I started to think what a bad
idea it was to submit my enfeebled body to such a severe test
just now. Supposing I died? Everyone would think it was damn
funny and they'd be right. I tried a little laugh, but the sight of
Chris's haggard face made me apprehensive. I shifted around
on the wall the way you do in bed when you're overtired, but
every position I found was as sickening as the last. Soon the
floor dropped away and the walls started spinning even faster.
My feet were pressed unnaturally outwards, my chin was

forced to the side. I saw the faces of the black girls looking expectantly down on us from the gallery and wondered horribly whether all this could possibly get any worse.

A boy next to me on the wall was loving every moment. He took off his coat, rolled from side to side, then got into a kneeling position, his head between his knees. Gradually he forced his body upright until it was sticking horizontally out from the wall, a smile all over his face. He lifted his arm to the girls and bowed, instantly crumbling into an upside down position on the wall.

By now my stomach had caved in and was trying to wrap itself round my backbone. How much had I paid for this fun therapy? God, I'd paid for Chris as well! It must be a punishment for something. I shouldn't have been so cruel to that PR. I couldn't believe it was only yesterday I'd felt so fit and randy. So *young*!

'I think I'm dying,' said Dr Feelgood's manager.

'So am I,' I said.

I looked up and saw the crowd of black teenagers like spectators in a freakshow, their faces alive with mildly sadistic glee as they poured their laughter over our suffering heads.

'Who's a pretty boy now?' I said to Chris as we crawled to freedom.

The Best in the World

Goodbye New York. Goodbye to all the names in my address book, Gilly and Sal whoever you are, Andrea and Mr Solomons, Nicky and Vicky and Howard. Goodbye to the Subway, the numbered streets which lead you on, Avenues which see you home, Central Park and the squirrels. Goodbye to Mrs Paul's Candied Sweet Potatoes, 'Almost Heaven' peanut butter, 'organic apples'. Goodbye to all the record shops I've wandered through in all the American towns. 'This guy tells me it's hand baggage,' said the porter at Kennedy, lifting my record-sack with difficulty. 'I pick it up and it weighs more 'n he does.' Goodbye American Jewish Princesses who talk like diamonds, Try-it-you'll-like-it girls who say everything is 'the-best-in-the-world' because it is, education executives who say 'quote-unquote' in case it isn't. Goodbye New York of the crouching paranoid veterans, the mad cyclist, the Wall Street saxophonist, graffiti cries. Your margin of madness is wider than that of other cities, like a wider sidewalk, a wider margin of error, and your citizens wander and cower and fight and dance in it. On 2nd Avenue I saw my dream walking. 'Hello, Dream,' I said. 'Get the hell, motherfucker,' said my dream.

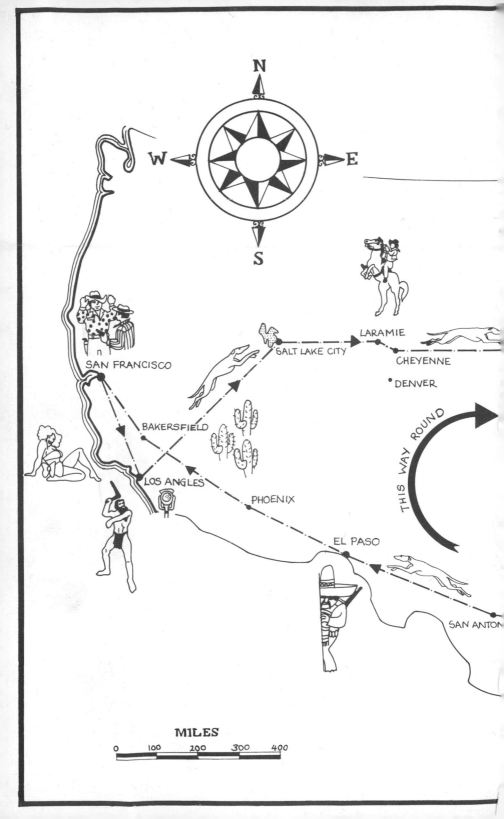